SNAPSHOTS OF THE 60s

SNAPSHOTS OF THE
60s

Brian Innes

REFERENCE GROUP
Brown

ISBN 1 84044 099 6

Produced by The Brown Reference Group
8 Chapel Place, Rivington Street, London EC2A 3DQ, UK
www.brownpartworks.co.uk

Editor: Henry Russell
Designer: Simon Webb
Picture Researcher: Adrian Bentley
Editorial Director: Lindsey Lowe
Art Director: Dave Goodman
Production Manager: Matt Weyland

Picture Credits

Corbis: Bettmann 10, 12, 18, 58, 62, 66, 72, 74, 88, 94, 98, 116, 132, 136, 144,
168, 172; Wally McNamee 134; Vittoriano Rastelli 64, 110; Flip Schulke 38, 100,
Ted Strechinsky 46, 124; Miroslav Zajic 154. **Hulton Archive**: 8, 14, 16, 26, 30, 32,
38, 40, 50, 52, 54, 56, 60, 68, 70, 76, 78, 80, 96, 108, 120, 122, 126, 142, 146,
158; Peter Ferrar 170; *The Observer* 102; Catherine Ursillo 160; Santi Visalli Inc.
130. **Robert Hunt Library**: 28, 48, 84, 90, 92, 104, 118, 128, 164. **NASA**: 34, 86,
162. **National Archives**: 24, 138, 140. **Popperfoto**: 150. **Private Eye**: 106. **TRH
Pictures**: 20, 82, 148. **Topham**: Alan Koss 174; Novosti 22.

Front cover (clockwise from top left): **Robert Hunt Library; Hulton Archive; Hulton
Archive; Corbis**: Bettmann; *The Observer;* **Hulton Archive**
Back cover (left to right): **Topham**: Novosti; **Hulton Archive**

Printed and bound in Hong Kong

1 2 3 4 5   06 05 04 03 02

Contents

Introduction

It was early spring 1960. As associate editor of a glossy printing trade monthly, I was in West Berlin, surrounded on all sides by the German People's Republic, well within the Russian sphere of influence. I was on my way to the annual Leipzig Trade Fair, even further to the east. I had applied for accreditation papers, and had been told that I would have to pick them up at the Fair offices in East Berlin.

At the time the West German mark was—officially or unofficially, I forget—worth at least four times its East German relative. Every day, manual workers crossed over from East Berlin to the West, earning what to them was a small fortune before returning home. East German security police, the "Vopos," made frequent checks, turning unfortunates off the U-Bahn, the overground railway that still ran between the two halves of the city, but the traffic continued.

My hotel was at the end of the Kurfürstendamm. It was early evening: my little map suggested that the Leipzig Fair offices were only a short walk away. So I set out to find them. As I walked, I realized that I had left my passport in my room—but no one challenged me as I crossed into the East.

In due course I found the Fair offices; and then I had to make my return to freedom. Due west, the Unter den Linden avenue stretched straight to the Brandenburg Gate, the frontier. It was nearly dark, and beginning to rain. Vopos in capes, submachine guns slung over their shoulders, prowled back and forth. Putting my faith in my nationality—and my innocence—I strode steadily forward. Again, nobody asked for my papers, and soon, with a huge sigh of relief, I passed under the looming black shadow of the Gate, and reached my hotel.

Fifteen months later, construction of the Berlin Wall divided the city into two halves. Over the next 28 years many lost their lives trying to cross to the West.

That Berlin experience colored all my responses to the 1960s. At first, it seemed that the Cold War was a standoff between East and West. But then came the Cuban missile crisis, American intervention in Vietnam, violent antiwar demonstrations, the emergence of "flower power," and student unrest. The word "revolution" was heard on all sides, but the change was not seen for some time.

At a more mundane level, but one that almost immediately affected everyday life, came startling revolutions in popular music, fashion, and sex. Modern popular music is now commonly thought to have begun with The Beatles, but the seeds had been sown some years earlier. During most of the 1950s, the music known as "pop" largely comprised gentle ballads or jolly songs from shows, performed by men in formal suits and women in demure dresses. There was, admittedly, also "rhythm 'n' blues"—but that was heard only on small local radio stations in the United States, while, in Europe, it was available only as rare specialist "race" recordings. The rock 'n' roll breakthrough came in 1955, when the charts were stormed by jean-wearing, hip-swiveling Elvis Presley.

The transition was, nevertheless, gradual. For the next eight years, the charts were dominated by the likes of Frank Sinatra and Tony Bennett. In Britain, Cliff Richard, a pale imitator of Presley, proved an instant success in 1958. My own band, The Temperance Seven, played 1930s' jazz-style dance music and kept Cliff Richard out of the Number 1 spot for many weeks in 1961. But then came The Beatles and The Rolling Stones, who changed for ever the course of Western pop.

Fashion and sex went hand in hand. The contraceptive pill was put on sale in 1962, and women who had previously worn broad skirts and petticoats were suddenly strutting confidently in miniskirts and knee-high boots. Historians will tell you that the miniskirt was launched in France in 1965, but it had appeared much earlier in Britain. As early as 1958 impoverished art students had bought scraps of fabric from the ends of rolls, and stitched them into skirts and dresses that ended, inevitably, above the knees.

The least attractive aspect of the 1960s was the "drug culture." In the first few years of the decade mind-bending drugs such as LSD and mescalin remained legally available, and they were used by the new rock musicians, as well as by the political "underground." As a result, it is said that if you can remember the 1960s, you weren't there. Well, I was there, and I remember them.

Brian Innes

The Sharpeville Massacre

March 21, 1960: in a moment of quiet after violence, men, women, and young children lie dead, dying, and wounded on a South African street, mowed down by police bullets. Their belongings are strewn around them: there is not a single weapon in sight. What had they done to provoke such a violent response?

Residents of Sharpeville, near Johannesburg, had marched to protest the injustice of apartheid, the policy of separate development for blacks and whites that had been codified by the white Afrikaner Nationalist Party in 1948. Under the repressive rules of the system, ownership of land by Africans was limited to "Bantu Homelands" (native reserves), and Africans were made to obtain permission before entering urban areas. Sexual relations and marriage between whites and nonwhites were illegal. The right to vote, which in any case was restricted to men, was denied to nonwhites. Many skilled occupations were reserved exclusively for white workers. As in the southern United States at that time, there was strict racial segregation in every aspect of daily life.

Sharpeville was held up by the South African government as a model of a black township, an advert for the success of separate development—some of the homes even had running water. When the inhabitants took to the streets, the authorities' response was swift and brutal—they feared rebellion, and insubordination would not be tolerated. The police opened fire on the crowd, killing 69 and injuring 178.

The massacre had lasting consequences. Abroad, there was outrage and widespread condemnation; within South Africa, the African National Congress (A.N.C.), which had previously opposed violence, now abandoned its policy of passive resistance. "Is it politically correct to continue preaching peace and non-violence," asked 33-year-old Nelson Mandela, "when dealing with a government whose barbaric practices have brought so much suffering and misery to Africans?"

There were further clashes between Africans and police. The government imposed martial law, and outlawed the A.N.C. Mandela went underground, encouraging sabotage of state and military targets, but was arrested in 1964 and thrown in jail, where he remained for more than 27 years.

These unarmed black people were shot in the back while running away from South African security forces determined to break up a peaceful demonstration.

Brazil's New Capital City

The National Congress, with its stark twin towers, is the symbol of Brasilia. These were the buildings that appeared in press and publicity coverage of the opening of the city that was custom-built to replace Rio de Janeiro as the capital of Brazil.

The idea of a new city in the interior of Brazil had been mooted as early as 1763. The plan was to use it as a base from which to exploit the surrounding land's largely untapped natural resources, especially timber from the Amazon rain forest and a host of valuable minerals. Nothing was done until 1955, on the inauguration of Juscelino Kubitschek de Oliveira. The new president—whose campaign slogan had been "fifty years' development in five"—decreed the construction of a completely new capital on a remote plateau nearly 600 miles northwest of Rio de Janeiro, the long-established seat of government. Kubitschek himself turned the first sod in 1957 and, despite the difficulties involved in access to the site, the new city—although far from completed—was opened with much ceremony in 1960.

Lucia Costa, a leading Brazilian architect, produced the ground plan for Brasilia—which has since been described as "a model of geometrical simplicity whose beauty is (unfortunately) best appreciated from the air." It is laid out in the form of a bow and arrow (although some have likened it to an airplane), the arrow forming the 5-mile-long Avenida Monumental that culminates in a cathedral and the seat of government. Costa's assistant, Oscar Niemeyer, drafted grandiose plans for the principal buildings, which included the lakeside presidential palace and the Brasilia Palace Hotel. As work progressed, however, it became apparent that some of the most fantastic designs were impracticable, and these had to be simplified during the course of construction.

Residents of Rio de Janeiro naturally considered Brasilia an extravagant folly, but most Brazilians accepted the city as an apt symbol of their future prosperity. Yet despite all the good intentions, Brasilia is now regarded as a sociological failure. Squalid slums of shanties have grown up on the outskirts of the city, because insufficient cheap housing was built to accommodate those who moved to the area, but who then failed to profit from Brazil's "economic miracle."

The National Congress building shortly before its formal opening. The photograph captures the brief moment between the departure of the construction crews and the arrival of the people.

U-2 Spyplane

On May 1, 1960 U.S. pilot Gary Powers took off from a secret base in Pakistan on what he expected to be a routine spying mission over the Soviet Union. Reconnaissance flights such as this had been taking place since 1956—the Russians knew about them, but for years lacked the technology to intercept the state-of-the-art Lockheed U-2 spyplanes that flew at heights of up to 90,000 feet, had a range of 6,400 miles, and were equipped with sensitive electronic equipment, and high-definition cameras that, according to the manufacturers, the Fairchild Corporation, were "capable of distinguishing the rivets on a Russian tank."

On this day, however, a recently developed Russian long-range missile brought down Powers's plane near Sverdlovsk. It was only a few weeks before a summit conference was due to be held in Paris, France, in an attempt to ease the rigors of the Cold War, and the incident brought relations between the Soviet Union and the United States to a new low.

The downing of the U-2 was made public by Soviet premier Nikita Khrushchev on May 5. The White House attempted to explain away the disaster, indignantly claiming that the aircraft was a civilian plane, carrying out meteorological research over Turkey, and that it had accidentally strayed into Soviet airspace (which hardly explained how it had been brought down 1,200 miles inside the Russian border). But all their blustering came to nought when Khrushchev revealed that Powers had escaped by parachute, been captured, and had confessed. Urgently, U.S. president Dwight D. Eisenhower promised that all U-2 flights would be suspended, but this was insufficient to save the Paris Summit. Khrushchev even proposed that the President should be impeached.

The remains of Power's plane and his equipment—including the "suicide needle" with which he was supposed to give himself a lethal injection if captured, but which he had omitted to use—were put on display in Moscow. In a trial that was broadcast across the world, the pilot was found guilty of espionage and sentenced to 10 years' imprisonment. On February 10, 1962, however, Powers was exchanged for Russian spy Rudolph Abel, who had been arrested in the United States in 1955.

Gary Powers stands in the dock behind his attorney, Mikhail Grinev, as he is sentenced by a Soviet court for espionage.

Kennedy versus Nixon

The turning point of the 1960 U.S. presidential election campaign—the two candidates, Democrat John Fitzgerald Kennedy and Republican Richard Milhous Nixon, take part in a series of four debates televised across the nation and watched by 70 million people. This was the first time the medium had been used in a major political contest, and the broadcasts probably determined the result of a close race.

In many ways an unlikely candidate, 43-year-old Kennedy was the scion of a prosperous Boston Roman Catholic family of Irish ancestry, who contrasted with the predominantly Anglo-Saxon Protestants of the U.S. upper echelons. He was a senator, but not a distinguished one, and had a weak record on civil rights. However, he had fought heroically in World War II, and displayed a wealth of charm. He cleverly exploited his background, meeting anti-Catholic prejudice face-to-face, and winning public enthusiasm for his beautiful wife, Jacqueline. Above all, Kennedy had lavish funding provided by his father Joseph, a former U.S. ambassador to Britain.

Nixon was a 47-year-old lawyer who had played a major role in the anti-Communist "witch-hunts" of the early 1950s, and was the incumbent vice-president in the outgoing administration of Dwight D. Eisenhower. His reputation for deviousness was reflected in the nickname "Tricky Dicky."

In the debates, Kennedy stood confidently tall and handsome. Nixon looked haggard and ill at ease—he was still weak from a recent illness, perspired heavily under the studio lights, and had heavy five-o'clock shadow that made him appear shifty. While most viewers felt that the Democrat had regularly scored points against his adversary, many who listened to the debate on radio—and therefore heard only the arguments, without seeing the candidates—reached the opposite conclusion. But the die was cast. Straight after the broadcasts, Kennedy's popularity soared in the polls. One Southern senator said, disapprovingly, that the Democrat combined the qualities of Franklin D. Roosevelt and Elvis Presley. It was a winning combination. On November 8, Kennedy took 303 electoral votes to Nixon's 219, albeit with only a narrow margin of some 118,000 popular votes.

John F. Kennedy (right) faces Richard M. Nixon across the studio floor during the first U.S. presidential election to have been covered—and influenced—by television.

The *Lady Chatterley* Trial

Straight after an historic British court verdict, a man allows himself to be photographed with a novel that had long been banned for obscenity, and which no one would previously have dared be seen reading in public.

Lady Chatterley's Lover was written by English author D. H. Lawrence, and privately printed in Florence, Italy, in 1928. Far from his best work, it became notorious: Lawrence's preoccupation with sex, and his use of "four-letter words," had already gained him a bad reputation when *The Rainbow* was seized by police and declared obscene in 1915, and *Lady Chatterley's Lover* suffered the same fate. Smuggled copies, published by the Travellers' Companion Library in Paris, France, in the 1950s, were regularly seized by British and U.S. customs, and in 1955 a London bookseller was sentenced to two months' imprisonment for stocking the book.

Two critical events occurred on July 21, 1959. In Britain, the backbench Labor M.P. Roy Jenkins saw the passage into law of his Obscene Publications Act, which for the first time allowed the defense of "literary merit" to be used against charges of obscenity. In the United States, the Grove Press won an action to allow an unexpurgated edition of *Lady Chatterley's Lover* to be distributed by mail, the U.S. Court of Appeals ruling, some months later, that "this is a major and distinguished novel, and Lawrence one of the great writers of the age."

In 1960, to celebrate the 30th anniversary of Lawrence's death, Penguin Books issued eight of his works, including a complete *Lady Chatterley*. The English Director of Public Prosecutions brought a test case, which came to trial at the Old Bailey in November. Defense witnesses made sweeping and sometimes ludicrous claims for the book's literary merit. The Bishop of Woolwich, for example, described the adultery between Lady Chatterley and her gamekeeper as "an act of holy communion." However, prosecuting counsel Mervyn Griffith-Jones earned lasting ridicule when he asked the jury: "Would you approve of your young sons, young daughters—because girls can read as well as boys—reading this book?.... Is this a book you would even wish your wife or your servants to read?" The jury found for the defense, and Penguin sold nearly two million copies of the book within a year.

The day after after an English court found that Lady Chatterley's Lover *was fit to be read in public, a man on the London Underground revels a little selfconsciously in his new freedom.*

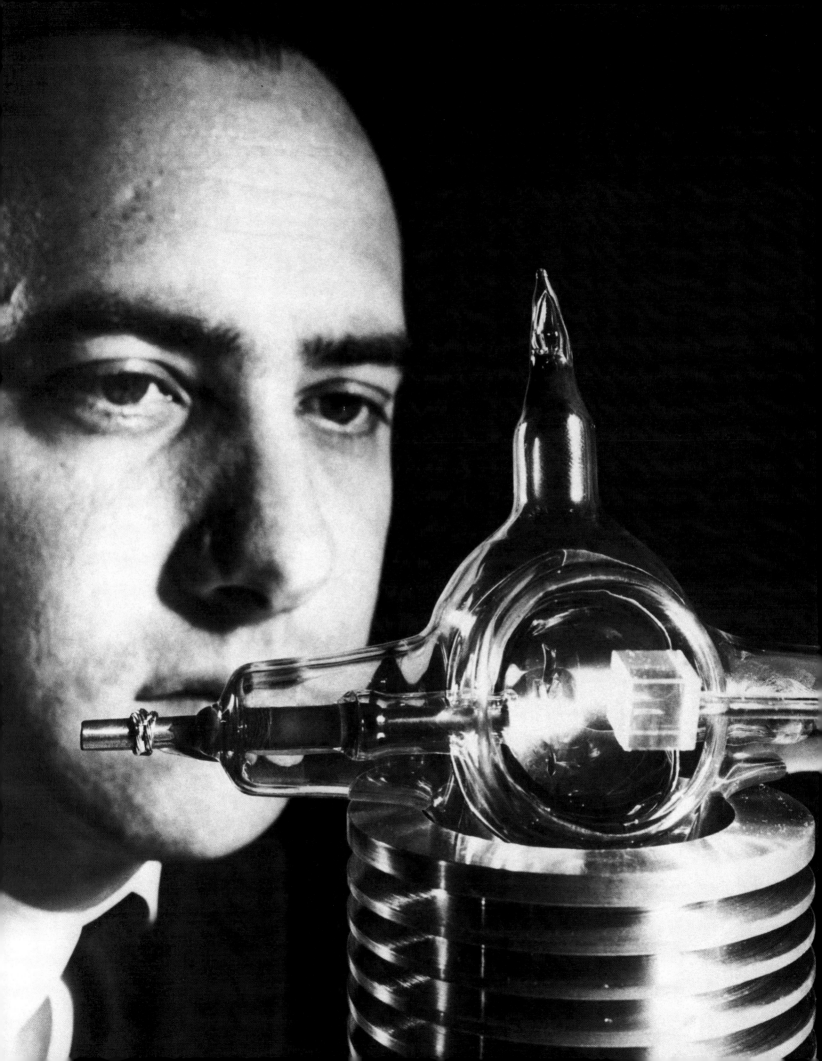

The First Laser

Lasers are now a familiar part of everyday life. CD players, bar-code readers, radar detectors, and computer printers all depend on them. Glass fiber-optic cables transmit telephone, television, and computer signals by laser, and in eye and brain surgery a laser incision can inflict less damage than a scalpel. In industry, a laser beam can weld steel, or drill hundreds of minute holes in the head of a pin. And the laser has been used to measure astronomical distance.

The basic principle of laser technology was proposed by Albert Einstein in 1917, and the first practical application, the maser (an acronym for "microwave amplification by stimulated electromagnetic radiation"), was made in 1954 by Nobel laureate Charles Townes. Four years later, Townes, now working at Columbia University with his brother-in-law Arthur Schawlow, wrote a paper on the principles of the laser, the "l" standing for "light." The name had been coined by Gordon Gould, a postgraduate student at Columbia.

However, it was Theodore Maiman, a physicist at the Hughes Research Laboratories in Miami, Florida, who won the race to construct the first operational laser. Maiman used the filament of a powerful lamp, wrapped round a ruby crystal, to stimulate the chromium atoms in the gemstone, and thus produced a focused beam of red light of a single wavelength. The narrow beam was so concentrated that it could raise the temperature of the spot on which it was focused higher than that of the Sun.

Since Maiman's great breakthrough, further developments have made it possible to control the power in the beam, and it is this that has made the laser so important in surgery. At high power, the beam will vaporize tissue cells, and so cut through them; at lower power, it will merely kill the cells.

Unlike rays of ordinary light, laser beams do not spread out, and therefore travel at a constant speed. Because of this property, they have been used to determine the distance between Earth and the Moon by measuring the time taken for laser pulses to bounce back off reflectors left on the Moon's surface by American astronauts.

Maiman patented the laser in 1960 at the age of 42. In honor of his achievement, 24 years later he was inducted into the National Inventors' Hall of Fame.

On July 7, 1960, Dr. Theodore Maiman poses behind the cube-shaped ruby crystal that he had used to make the first laser.

Death of Lumumba

On June 30, 1960, the Belgian Congo—an African colony founded in 1885 by King Leopold II, largely for his own enrichment—was suddenly granted independence from Belgium without any preparation for the transfer of power. Joseph Kasavubu became president, and his nationalist rival Patrice Emergy Lumumba was elected prime minister of the new republic.

A massive crisis developed immediately due to ethnic and political conflicts. Five days later the infant nation's army mutinied, and Belgium sent troops back into the country. On July 11, the people of Katanga (now Shaba) province, backed by white European settlers, declared independence from the republic. Determined to crush the secession, Lumumba appealed first to the United Nations (U.N.), and then to the Soviet Union for military aid. The Congo severed relations with Belgium, a U.N. emergency force arrived on July 15, and Belgium was ordered to withdraw.

On September 2, the Soviet Union provided aircraft at Lumumba's request. Kasavubu disapproved of this action, so three days later he dismissed his prime minister. Still claiming to head the government, Lumumba was captured by Kasavubu's troops on December 2, and put under house arrest before being transferred to prison. Meanwhile a three-sided civil war raged between government troops under Colonel Joseph Mobutu (later Sese Seko Mobutu), others still loyal to Lumumba, and Katangan separatists under Moise-Kapenda Tshombe.

In January 1961, Lumumba was kidnapped from prison. No one knew who took him—some said it was the C.I.A., others that it was Belgian mercenaries. What is certain, however, is that Lumumba was then handed over to the Katangans, who murdered him. It was not until November 2001 that Belgium finally admitted the involvement of its then minister for African affairs, Count Harold d'Aspremont Lynden, in arrangements for the slaying. U.N. efforts to intervene in Katanga met with fierce opposition, and condemnation from the Soviet Union. On September 17, 1961, U.N. secretary general Dag Hammarskjöld was killed in an air crash on his way to meet Tshombe in Katanga, and rumors have persisted to the present day that the crash was no accident.

How are the mighty fallen—this snapshot shows Patrice Lumumba under armed guard in the back of a truck after his arrest. His death was announced on February 13, 1961.

Gagarin Orbits the Earth

Yuri Alexeyevitch Gagarin—once he had recovered from the immense thrust forces of takeoff—sent radio reports to base without apparent emotion. "The flight is proceeding normally... I feel well... I can see the Earth, it is covered with a blue mist...." Although the flight was guided automatically, Gagarin carried a sealed envelope containing the code to open a combination lock that would have enabled him to take control in an emergency.

One hour and 48 minutes after his 9.07 a.m. blastoff, Moscow time, having circled the Earth at a maximum height of 203 miles, Gagarin landed in a Russian field near the banks of the Volga River. Moscow claimed that Gagarin landed Vostok 1 himself, but experts agree that he must have parachuted out at about 23,000 feet.

The Soviet Union had been leading the "space race" against the United States since 1957. On October 4 of that year, it had launched Sputnik 1 into orbit. The craft was visible in the night sky, and audible by radio as it constantly "beeped." Just one month later, the dog Laika survived several orbits of the Earth, and in August 1960 two dogs were successfully launched, and recovered unharmed. It was with this experimental experience behind them that the Russians decided to put a man into space, and former test pilot Gagarin was the chosen one.

News of the latest Soviet success was received with rage in Washington, D.C. In a frantic effort to restore national pride, Commander Alan Shepherd Jr. was bundled aboard Freedom 7, and hurled into space on May 5; but his suborbital flight lasted a mere 15 minutes, and could not compare with Gagarin's achievement. On May 25, President Kennedy announced a space program "which promises dramatic results in which we could win," and vowed that America would put a man on the Moon before the end of the decade.

A modest man, Yuri Gagarin was acclaimed a Soviet hero. Streets were named after him, and monuments were erected to commemorate his achievement. Sadly, he subsequently became a heavy drinker, and was killed in a plane crash in 1968, just one year before the American Neil Armstrong stepped out on to the surface of the Moon to fulfil President Kennedy's prophesy.

Yuri Gagarin in the capsule of Vostok 1 on the morning of April 12, 1961, when the 27-year-old Soviet cosmonaut became the first man to make an orbital space flight around the Earth.

The Bay of Pigs Fiasco

When Fidel Castro seized power in Cuba on the first day of 1959, he predicted that the United States would soon try to crush his anti-imperialist revolution, and he promised that the invaders would be bloodily defeated. His prediction, and his promise, came true in little more than two years.

On April 17, 1961, some 1,500 right-wing anti-Castro Cuban exiles, trained by the C.I.A. and carrying American weapons, were landed on Playa Girón in the Bay of Pigs by American vessels. The exodus of thousands of Cubans to the United States had persuaded the C.I.A. that the invasion would set off a mass uprising against Castro. But the Cuban leader's sweeping reforms—free medical care, literacy training, housing programs, land-ownership changes, the closure of Havana's casinos and brothels, and the promise of racial and sexual equality—had been welcomed by the impoverished majority. The imposition of a U.S. economic blockade had served only to unite the Cuban people against a common foe.

The attempted invasion was a disaster: the landing beach was badly chosen, communications were patchy, and orders for successive flights of supporting USAF planes remained unsigned by President Kennedy. Within three days, 400 of the invaders were dead, and the rest had surrendered. "We look," said one U.S. commentator, writing in the *New York Times*, "like fools to our friends, rascals to our enemies, and incompetents to the rest."

Kennedy had approved the operation—based on a plan inherited from the outgoing Eisenhower administration—reluctantly, but he shouldered the blame for the fiasco. He promised the imprisoned rebels that one day they would again be in charge in Cuba. Eventually, however, the United States had to pay a ransom of $53 million-worth of food and medicine to secure their release. Castro then announced that he was aligning his policy with that of the Soviet Union, and that Cuba was to be run on strictly communist principles. "I have been a Marxist-Leninist all along," he declared, "and will remain one until I die."

Forty years later, at the dawn of a new millennium, Cuba still remained economically isolated from the United States.

A Cuban soldier guards proof positive of U.S. complicity in the Bay of Pigs—the wreckage of an American B26 bomber, one of six shot down, crudely disguised in Cuban livery.

Eichmann Trial

Adolf Eichmann was one of the chief architects of the Final Solution, the Nazi plan to exterminate every Jew in Europe during World War II. After the defeat of Germany in 1945 he disappeared, and for years no one knew if he was even alive.

Then, in the fall of 1959, Nazi hunters received a tip that Eichmann was working as a mechanic for Mercedes-Benz in Buenos Aires, Argentina, under the name of Ricardo Klement. Israel sent agents of their secret service, Mossad, who kept the suspect under surveillance for months. They went to great lengths to satisfy themselves that he was who they thought he was, and then, having done so, on May 11, 1960, they grabbed Eichmann as he got off a bus on his way home from work, and took him to a safe house for detailed questioning.

The Mossad agents drugged him and smuggled him out of Argentina to Israel. For 11 months after his capture, Eichmann was held in a remote top-security prison, and interrogated by investigators who were building the case against him. Such was the mass of evidence that the Israeli police had to set up a whole new department to deal with it. This was known as Bureau 06, and it was staffed chiefly by German-speaking officers. Israel wanted to ensure that no one tried to free Eichmann or kill him, and extraordinary security precautions were taken to prevent him being assassinated, escaping or committing suicide. Even anti-aircraft weapons were installed at the compound.

The trial opened in Jerusalem on April 11, 1961. The whole proceedings were filmed by the American Capital Cities Broadcasting Corporation, thus making it the first trial ever to be televised, and one of the first events to be videotaped. Security was very tight. Eichmann himself sat in a bulletproof glass booth.

The last evidence was heard in August. The court then adjourned for four months to consider its verdict. On December 11, the three judges found Eichmann guilty on all charges. The Nazi war criminal was sentenced to death and hanged in Ramleh Prison on May 31, 1962. It was decided that no grave would mark his life and that he would have no resting place in Israel. His ashes were scattered over the Mediterranean Sea in international waters.

Adolf Eichmann is examined by an Israeli prison doctor to make sure that he is fit to stand trial for the murder of six million Jews.

Nureyev Defects

Rudolf Nureyev was just 23 years old when he made a wild jump over a railing at Orly Airport in Paris, France, and asked for political asylum.

Born in Irkutsk, Siberia, on March 17, 1938, and of Tatar descent, Nureyev was regarded as one of the Soviet Union's most promising young dancers. He had revealed an independent spirit from an early age, refusing to join the Young Communists. He later turned down a place at the Bolshoi Ballet on the grounds that it was too restrictive in its conventions, and instead joined Leningrad's Kirov Ballet, where he soon became a star. But even there he was critical of the ballet's artistic policy and the abilities of fellow members of the company. During a European tour with the Kirov, Nureyev preferred to spend his free time fraternizing with foreigners. Such practices were frowned on by the Soviet authorities; when he learnt that he was being sent back to Moscow to be disciplined he made his leap for freedom on June 17, 1961.

The news of Nureyev's defection from the Soviet Union made great propaganda, and was welcomed with enthusiasm by ballet fans in the West. Within a few days, Nureyev had become one of the highest-paid dancers in Europe, starring as the principal male in *The Sleeping Beauty* for the Marquis de Cuevas Ballet in Paris. From there he moved to London, England, as permanent guest artiste with the Royal Ballet. He soon became the favorite partner of Britain's leading ballerina, Margot Fonteyn (pictured with him here). Together they won the adulation of ballet fans: one ecstatic audience in Vienna, Austria, awarded them 89 curtain calls for a reworking of *Swan Lake* in 1964.

Nureyev never became a permanent member of a major dance troupe in the West, preferring to work with various companies for short runs only. His technical ability and moody personality brought inevitable comparisons with another Russian of the previous generation, the legendary Vaslav Nijinsky. Like Nijinsky, Nureyev also ventured into choreography, devising and performing routines with nearly every major ballet company in the world. Rudolf Nureyev died on January 6, 1993, reportedly of an AIDS-related illness.

After his defection, Russian ballet dancer Rudolf Nureyev clearly revels in the freedom to dress as he wishes and do what he likes—opportunities that were denied to him in his native land.

The Berlin Wall

Five days after a barbed-wire barrier was hastily erected across central Berlin by East German soldiers during the night of August 12–13, 1961, Soviet tanks trained their guns on West Berlin to protect the concrete wall that was then being built to make the division more permanent. The barbed wire was replaced in stages by a concrete wall 10 to 15 feet high that eventually ran for 28 miles around the whole of the Western sector of the city.

East German soldiers kept constant guard on the Berlin Wall from fortified watchtowers along its length, and shot anyone who attempted to climb it. Escape into West Berlin from East Germany became even more hazardous after the installation of minefields. The "Iron Curtain" predicted by Winston Churchill in his famous 1946 speech at Fulton, Missouri, had become a reality.

The Berlin Wall was put up to stem the flow of workers from the communist East to the democratic West. In the first seven months of 1961 alone, nearly a quarter of a million refugees had crossed into the free parts of the city, and the East German authorities decided to take drastic action.

The problem had been caused by the conditions imposed on Germany after its defeat in World War II. The nation had been split into four sections, each occupied by one of the victorious Allied powers—Britain, France, the Soviet Union, and the United States. This division was mirrored in Berlin, but the former capital was located deep in the heart of the Soviet part of Germany. Tension between East and West first reached a crisis in June 1948, when the Western powers introduced a new currency, the Deutschmark, for West Germany. The Russians responded by blockading all land communications with West Berlin, and declaring East Germany, the Soviet zone of occupation, a sovereign state, the German Democratic Republic. The only way the western sectors could be kept supplied was by three air "corridors." West Berlin was kept going by a continuous airlift of millions of tons of supplies, until a year later the Russians agreed to lift their blockade.

The Berlin Wall stood for 28 years, during which several thousand people lost their lives, or were captured and imprisoned, in attempts to cross from East to West.

An historic snapshot at the junction of Zimmerstrasse and Friedrichstrasse, soon to be the site of Checkpoint Charlie, the most famous crossing point between the two sides of divided Berlin.

Algerian Independence

Cheering citizens gathered in the streets of Algiers to celebrate their newly acquired independence from France in 1962, one of the key moments in the decline of France as a colonial power.

The European nation had been economically weakened by World War II, and had endured 26 changes of government in 14 years. It had lost Indo-China in the summer of 1954, and then, in November, Algeria's National Liberation Front (F.L.N.) declared a revolution. Neighboring Morocco and Tunisia were also agitating for independence, which they obtained in 1956, but there was a difference: they were protectorates; Algeria was part of Metropolitan France, and its Muslim population of nearly nine million—together with the colonial *pieds-noirs*, born of French ancestry—were legally French citizens. More importantly, from an economic point of view, oil had recently been discovered in the country's desert interior.

France responded with unparalleled ferocity. By 1956, French troops in the country numbered nearly a half a million; villagers were driven out of F.L.N.-held areas into resettlement camps. The F.L.N. retaliated with a campaign of terrorist bombing. In 1957, the revelation that French General Jacques Massu's troops had regularly tortured prisoners in Algiers led to a massive swing in French popular opinion, and Algerian independence now seemed a possibility. The French army, however, rebelled; Massu was named chief of the uprising, and he called on retired General Charles de Gaulle to come to the rescue. De Gaulle accepted the offer of the French premiership, then the presidency, and then visited Algiers, where he assured the colonists: *"Je vous ai compris"* ("I have understood you").

What he understood, however, was that colonialism was no longer sustainable. But the F.L.N. rejected his reforming proposals, and continued their guerrilla war. In 1960, facing the probability of Algerian independence, the *pieds-noirs* also rioted; however, a referendum in January 1961, held in France, Algeria, and other French overseas territories, passed a strong vote for Algerian self-determination. An uneasy peace was eventually established with the F.L.N., and on July 3, 1962 the independence of Algeria was declared.

Supporters acclaim the election of Ahmed ben Bella, who became the first prime minister of independent Algeria in 1962, and president the following year.

Telstar

Telstar under construction at the Bell Telephone Laboratory in New Jersey. Despite the satellite's small size (only 32 inches in diameter), and low weight (175 pounds), it made a giant impact on global telecommunications.

Telstar was launched on July 10, 1962, by a Delta rocket from Cape Canaveral, Florida, and followed an elliptical orbit from 500 to 3,500 miles above the surface of the Earth. Using solar power, it amplified faint television signals 10 billion times, and beamed them back to ground stations.

The successful launch caused great excitement. Later that same day, viewers gathered round television sets for what was advertised as the event of the century— the first direct, live pictures transmitted between the United States and Europe. But the results were not in themselves impressive: fuzzy, broken-up pictures of the Stars and Stripes flying over the American Telephone and Telegraph Company (AT&T) building in Maine, greetings from the French actor Yves Montand interrupted by vision loss and crackling sound....

Nevertheless, the future of communications satellites was assured. In the United States, there was fierce argument over whether the government should control a high-orbit system of satellites to cover the globe, or whether AT&T, which had paid NASA to launch Telstar, should be allowed to develop its proposed low-orbit system. The Kennedy administration, faced with the expectation of immediate Soviet competition, gave the go-ahead to AT&T. Later that year, British pop group The Tornados achieved instant chart-topping success, in both Britain and the United States, with their recording of the instrumental single "Telstar."

Today, hundreds of artificial satellites orbit the Earth. Television, radio, telephone, and computer data can now be received from satellite in every quarter of the globe; navigational satellites enable one's position on the Earth's surface to be determined to within an accuracy of 10 yards; and weather satellites make meteorological forecasting more reliable than ever before.

Telstar was taken out of service on February 21, 1963, after some of its transistors were damaged by high-altitude radiation from the explosion of an atomic bomb.

Telstar was made of multifaceted aluminum spheroids with magnesium frames, and powered by 3,600 solar cells on the outside structure, and nickel-cadmium batteries inside.

Monroe Dies

On the morning of August 5, 1962, Marilyn Monroe's housekeeper discovered the body of the actress at her Los Angeles home, an empty bottle of sedatives at her bedside. She was just 36 years old, and at the height of her fame. "For the entire world," said her acting tutor Lee Strasberg in her funeral address, "she was a symbol of the eternal feminine."

Born Norma Jean Baker in 1926, Marilyn Monroe had fought hard to reach stardom: from nude calendar photos in 1948, followed by bit parts in the films *Love Happy* (1949) and *All About Eve* (1950), in a single year she played leading roles in three features—*Niagara*, *Gentlemen Prefer Blondes*, and *How to Marry a Millionaire* (all 1953). Eight other successful films followed, out of which *Some Like It Hot* (1959) has remained her lasting memorial.

But Monroe was never satisfied with her "dizzy blonde" image, its impermanence and lack of dignity. She strove constantly to achieve respectability through marriage, first to baseball star Joe DiMaggio, and subsequently to intellectual playwright Arthur Miller, and as an actress, studying under Strasberg at the Actors Studio. However, she continued to earn herself a reputation for erratic and unprofessional behavior: Billy Wilder, the director of *Some Like It Hot*, was quoted as telling the rest of the cast that they must be perfect in every take—because the first time Monroe got her lines right he would print it.

By the time *The Misfits* was finished in 1961, Monroe was a sorry victim of alcohol and prescribed drugs. The film's director, John Huston, warned: "In a while she'll either be dead or in a mental institution." In these circumstances her demise was sadly predictable, but it sparked off a wealth of conspiracy theories. Her sex life was posthumously revealed to have been as erratic as her acting career: President Kennedy was widely believed to have been one of her lovers, and the movements of Kennedy's brother-in-law, the actor Peter Lawford, on the night of her death, have never been fully or satisfactorily explained.

Monroe's memory lives on. For some, she is a symbol of exploited womanhood; for most, however, she remains as she was in life—"the blonde goddess."

Monroe looking radiant at the 1962 Golden Globe ceremony in Hollywood, where she was presented with an award for being "World Film Favorite." A few months later she was dead.

James Meredith

By the summer of 1962, the movement to end segregation in the southern United States was gaining impetus. One of the staunchest bastions of white exclusivity was Mississippi University at Oxford, Mississippi—popularly known as "Ole Miss." When the prominent young black activist James H. Meredith applied for enrolment there, reaction was swift and hostile. The university at first refused to admit him, until ordered to do so by a Federal court. Even then, State Governor Ross Barnett resisted Meredith's enrolment, calling on whites to oppose the civil rights' movement, and declaring that this was "the moment of our greatest crisis since the war between the states."

With a bodyguard of Federal marshals, Meredith attempted to make a low-key arrival on campus on September 27, 1962, but he was greeted by a crowd throwing rocks and bottles. The violence quickly escalated. President Kennedy appeared on national television, appealing for restraint, but the racist mob rioted, resulting in two deaths and 160 injured marshals. It was only when Federal troops were called in that an uneasy peace was restored.

Ironically, white students at the university who made friendly approaches to Meredith suffered even greater harassment than he himself. One was forced to leave, and the parents of another were driven to issue a statement that he had suffered a nervous breakdown, and so could not be held responsible for his actions. In October, the American Association of University Professors issued a statement in which they claimed that "the deplorable events which took place... would not have occurred if the political authorities of the State had supported the University in adhering to the law of the land and its academic obligations." This was particularly mealy-mouthed in view of the way in which the university had originally attempted to block the young man's enrolment.

James Meredith successfully graduated from "Ole Miss" in 1963, and devoted his energies to the civil rights' movement. In June 1966, he led a Freedom March from Tennessee into Mississippi, during the course of which a white Mississippian fired a load of shotgun pellets into his back—but, fortunately, he survived.

Accompanied by Federal law enforcement officers, James Meredith attempts to step onto the campus of the University of Mississippi, but finds his way blocked by the lieutenant governor.

India versus China

An estimated 10,000 Indian soldiers and civilians died in the 1962 border clashes between India and China.

The region had long been the subject of bitter dispute. In 1913, Britain (which then controlled India), China, and Tibet reached an agreement that drew the frontier along the so-called McMahon Line, but this was later repudiated by the Chinese. After India achieved independence in 1947, the Chinese laid claim to a wide area south of the line. Their prime minister, Zhou Enlai, cited the evidence of a map in the 1929 edition of the *Encyclopedia Britannica*, which clearly showed the disputed area as Chinese!

India tried to maintain friendly relations with China, according it recognition in 1949, and consistently advocating its admission to the United Nations. However, the Indian government condemned the Chinese occupation of Tibet in 1950, and declared its determination to protect its border states.

In August 1959, a number of Chinese troops crossed the McMahon Line into northern Assam—a region then known as the North East Frontier Agency (N.E.F.A.), and now the state of Arunachal Pradesh—and captured an outpost at Longju. A visit by Zhou Enlai to New Delhi in April 1960 failed to resolve the dispute, and in October 1962 a much larger Chinese force invaded, extending its attack along the entire border, and penetrating deep into N.E.F.A. territory.

The Indian defenders were ordered not to withdraw, but they were relatively few in number, and the terrain was difficult and remote. Supplies and equipment had to be dropped by parachute, while the Chinese were only a few miles from their roadhead—and, above all, they had artillery. Fighting was fierce, and the Indians lost many killed or captured.

For a while it looked as if India and China would be drawn into a full-scale war. However, the Chinese found that their lines of communication were extended too far, and declared a unilateral ceasefire on November 21, withdrawing to the McMahon Line, but retaining a tract of territory the size of Switzerland. Today, China still claims about 36,000 square miles of Indian territory.

Women of the Indian Home Guard training in Tezpur in November 1962, when the whole of India went on alert during border clashes with China in Assam and Bhutan.

Cuban Missile Crisis

For a week in the fall of 1962, the Soviet Union and the United States teetered on the brink of war. Both nations had nuclear weapons, so many people feared the end of the world. This was the first time that the Soviets had deployed nuclear arms in the western hemisphere, and Russian ships—possibly carrying more missiles—were already known to be on their way to the Caribbean island of Cuba, only 90 miles from the American mainland.

There was near panic in Washington, as President Kennedy urgently consulted his advisers on what steps to take. Defense Secretary Robert McNamara was sanguine: "It makes no difference," he said, "whether you are killed by a missile fired from the Soviet Union or from Cuba." Others recommended an immediate invasion, but this was rejected because the previous attempt to take Cuba had ended in humiliation at the Bay of Pigs. In the end, Kennedy decided on a total naval blockade, and on October 22 he spoke on television, outlining the situation. "I have directed the armed forces," he announced, "to prepare for any eventuality."

For a week, the whole world anticipated the outbreak of an apocalyptic war. Khrushchev withdrew the Russian ships, but for some time he refused to allow Soviet engineers to dismantle the weapons that had already been installed in Cuba. The crisis intensified. Some 200,000 American troops gathered in Florida, and a U.S.A.F. pilot on a reconnaissance flight over the island was shot down and killed—he was, in fact, the only casualty of the confrontation.

Eventually, a compromise was reached. On October 28, the United States promised that it would never invade Cuba, and agreed to remove the nuclear missiles it had installed close to the Soviet border in Turkey—they were, in any case, Washington said, "obsolescent." In return, Khrushchev undertook to withdraw the weapons from Cuba. World—and possibly nuclear—war had been averted.

One important consequence of the crisis was the Limited Test-Ban Treaty, the brainchild of British prime minister Harold Macmillan, which was signed in 1964. Ratified by 100 nations—but not, at that time, China and France—it proscribed atmospheric, underwater, and space testing of nuclear weapons.

Members of the U.N. General Assembly look anxiously at still photographs of a Soviet ballistic missile site taken by a U.S. spyplane that had overflown Cuba on October 14, 1962.

Concorde Agreement

On November 29, 1962, French ambassador Geoffroy de Courcel and British aviation minister Julian Amery signed an historic agreement between their two nations to build the world's first supersonic commercial airplane.

The two companies that worked on the project, the British Aircraft Corporation and Sud-Aviation, undertook to have Concorde airborne by February 1968, but technical problems, and the constantly rising costs of production, made this impossible. The student riots in Paris in May 1968 were a further setback to French participation. Then the Soviet Union triumphantly put the supersonic Tupelev 144 into operation in December of that year. Opposition to Concorde was voiced not only in Britain and France, but also in the United States—American objections were particularly ominous, because transatlantic travel was the goal of Concorde's development. Environmentalists protested the inevitable noise pollution that the airplane would create, the damage that would be caused to buildings, health, and the ozone layer by its "sonic boom," and its huge fuel consumption.

Despite misgivings, the prototype finally took to the air in 1969. Two years later, the U.S. government cancelled funding for a supersonic aircraft being developed by Boeing, increasing doubts about Concorde's future. Eventually, in January 1976, nine Concordes went into service, flying from London and Paris to Bahrain, Caracas, Venezuela, and Washington, D.C., in British Airways and Air France livery, but hoped-for orders from other airlines were not forthcoming. Only after a 19-month legal battle, and the decision of the U.S. Supreme Court, was permission obtained to fly into New York. The first Concorde landed at John F. Kennedy International Airport on August 1, 1978. Yet supersonic air transportation never became a realistic business proposition, and Concorde remained a very expensive option for a privileged few.

Powered by four jet engines that produce 37,300 pounds of thrust, Concorde cruises at 1,320 m.p.h, almost twice the speed of sound (750 m.p.h. under standard atmospheric conditions). The futuristic airplane more than halved the flight time between London and New York.

De Courcel (left) and Amery sign the Concorde agreement. Behind them is a model of the airplane, showing its distinctive delta wings and pointed nose or "droop snoot."

Alcatraz Closes

Lying within San Francisco Bay, halfway between the Golden Gate and Oakland bridges and a little over a mile off the northern shore of the city, Alcatraz is a small island, some 12 acres of solid rock. For 30 years, it was one of the most formidable Federal prisons in the United States.

The original detention block on the island was built in 1912, and subsequently it became the U.S. Army's first long-term prison. The citizens of San Francisco objected to the ugly appearance of the stark buildings on the naked rock, and over the years vast consignments of soil were brought there, and flowers and bushes planted and tended by the inmates. In 1934, the Army handed over the island to the Department of Justice, and the military prison was converted into a high-security establishment for violent criminals, with tear-gas canisters permanently installed in the ceiling of the dining hall, and nearly 600 cells.

One of the first convicts to be incarcerated on Alcatraz, for some four years, was notorious Chicago gangster Al Capone, who was jailed on charges of tax evasion. Over the years, many hundreds of America's most brutal men were imprisoned on the island. Possibly the most famous inmate was Robert Stroud, a vicious killer who was transferred there after being in one prison after another since 1909. Sentenced to solitary confinement, he was allowed to breed nearly 300 birds in his isolated cell, and was the author of two books on canaries and their diseases. Thus he became known as "the Birdman of Alcatraz." Few men escaped from the prison buildings, and most were recaptured or shot on the shore of the island. Those who attempted to swim to liberty were either drowned, or eventually discovered, exhausted and suffering from hypothermia, and returned to the cells.

Because of its isolation—everything used there had to be shipped in—Alcatraz was nearly three times more expensive to operate than any other Federal prison, so the decision was taken to close it. Since it ceased to be a jail, the island and its buildings have become tourist attractions, with many boatloads of sightseers landing daily to inspect the facilities. Of particular interest to visitors are the Hole, a punishment cell, and the Strip Cell, in which prisoners were confined naked.

The last remaining inmates are escorted by guards to a boat for transfer to other prisons before the final closure of Alcatraz on March 21, 1963. Note the chains on the convicts' feet.

Birmingham, Alabama

Throughout the 1960s, continuing segregation of blacks and whites provoked bitter reactions, typified by the violence that accompanied James Meredith's admission to the University of Mississippi in 1962. The events that led to the violent confrontations in Birmingham, Alabama, began in February 1963, when, after months of wavering, President Kennedy announced his support for proposed federal legislation to establish, among other things, the right to vote, the right to education, the right to employment, and the desegregation of public facilities.

Then the charismatic civil rights leader, Martin Luther King, Jr., chose Birmingham as the next venue on his campaign of nonviolent protest. Shortly after his arrival in the city at Easter, 1963, he was arrested, and thrown into jail.

From his cell, King smuggled out his "Letter from Birmingham Jail," which defined his beliefs and contained the famous remark: "One who breaks an unjust law must do so openly, lovingly, and with a willingness to accept the penalty." Telephone calls from his wife to President Kennedy resulted in his rapid release, but on May 2 a thousand black children, marching in peaceful protest from their Baptist church into the downtown area, were arrested. The following day, as protests escalated, police chief Eugene "Bull" Connor sent in men with fire hoses, and unleashed dogs against the nonviolent demonstrators. Martin Luther King was again arrested, along with hundreds of others.

George Wallace, governor of Alabama, ordered state troopers to the assistance of the police, and the most violent confrontation took place on May 7. Kennedy intervened personally, threatening to send in troops if order was not restored. Local businessmen then agreed to the demands of the antisegregationist Southern Christian Leadership Conference, and an uneasy peace returned to the streets of the city. King declared the outcome a "great victory," but it did not yet promise security for black people. Bombings and attempted shootings increased in Birmingham, and spread throughout the South. However, news photographs such as this, together with liberal legislation by Washington, began to turn the tide of public opinion against segregation in the Southern states.

A police dog lunges at an African American demonstrator as state authorities try to break up a civil rights' demonstration in the segregated city of Birmingham, Alabama, in May 1963.

Skopje Earthquake

It was 5.17 a.m., local time, when a massive earthquake shook Skopje, the capital of Macedonia, then part of the Yugoslav Federation. For more than three hours, 80 shockwaves rocked the city. Skopje was almost totally destroyed: more than 1,000 inhabitants were killed, and nearly 200,000 left homeless. At that time, the old part of the city, dating from the Byzantine period, stood on a slope above the left bank of the Vardar River, overlooked by an ancient fortress. To the north stood a Roman aqueduct, and a Turkish stone bridge (miraculously preserved during the widespread devastation) crossed the river to the new quarter, begun in the 19th century but largely constructed after World War II.

The earthquake wiped out the waterfront, and the city's baroque National Theater. Thousands of proud municipal buildings and humble homes were reduced to rubble. Even as rescue workers began to scrabble among the daunting ruins, two aftershocks rumbled through the surrounding countryside. International aid came quickly, but Skopje had to be rebuilt from the ground up.

Fears of a future quake led some to recommend that the capital should be established elsewhere, but instead massive concrete slabs were set into the ground to provide protection against further tremors. Among the many international architects who took part in the reconstruction of Skopje was the Japanese urban planner Kenzo Tanga. He gave the center a "city wall" of high-rise apartment blocks, while the banks of the Vardar were laid out as tree-lined promenades. The rebuilding was followed by an influx of people from the surrounding countryside, who increased the population fivefold, and the new apartment blocks soon became unprepossessing slums.

Reconstruction was virtually completed by 1977. Modern Skopje is dominated by Soviet-style official buildings, already decaying; only the old trading quarter has been restored to its former glory. There are two great memorials to the horror of 1963: a commemorative museum stands on the site of the earthquake's epicenter, and, most poignantly, part of the ruined railroad station has been preserved, with the hands of its clock fixed forever at the fatal moment when the earth began to shake.

On July 26, 1963, the morning after the great natural disaster that shattered the city of Skopje, Yugoslavia, troops and workers search the ruins for survivors.

Great Train Robbery

Just before dawn on August 8, 1963, the driver of the night mail train from Glasgow, Scotland to London, England sighted an amber warning signal light up ahead. He slowed, and came to a stop at a red light in an isolated spot. The co-driver climbed down to the track to find a telephone—and was overpowered by two masked men. More men clambered into the cab, and coshed driver Jack Mills.

In the "traveling Post Office" coach postal workers, completely unaware of what was happening, continued sorting the mail. Behind their coach was a second car, packed with sacks full of banknotes, and beneath it another man was busy undoing the couplings that joined it to the rest of the train. Mills was dragged to his feet, and ordered to take the locomotive and the two coaches a further half-mile down the track to Cheddington, in Buckinghamshire, southern England. There, the masked robbers broke into the mail coach, terrifying the sorters, and manhandled 120 sacks of banknotes down the embankment and into a lorry and two ex-Army jeeps.

It was a brilliantly planned operation: the signal lights had been set by the simple expedient of connecting torch batteries to their terminals. The gang made off to nearby Leatherslade Farm. There they intended to lie low for several days; but when they heard on the radio that police were searching the surrounding countryside, they decided to disperse immediately, each carrying off some £150,000.

When police discovered the hideout, it was deserted, but the gang had carelessly removed their gloves inside the building, and fingerprint examinations revealed the identities of five well-known villains, who were soon rounded up, along with their accomplices. When the trial opened in January 1964, nine men stood in the dock; three more were still on the run, but were later captured. In addition, many people believe that another five members of the gang were never brought to justice.

In 1965, one gang member, Ronnie Biggs, coolly escaped from jail and disappeared. By the time British police located him in Brazil, he had fathered a child in his new country, and so could not be extradited. He remained at large until 2001, when, at the age of 71, he came home voluntarily for medical treatment, even though doing so meant that he would have to serve out the remainder of his 30-year sentence.

On the morning after the Great Train Robbery, the diesel locomotive still stands at the spot where its train was robbed of £2.5 million—at the time, the biggest robbery in British history.

"I Have A Dream"

Following their success in Birmingham, Alabama, in May 1963, the Reverend Dr. Martin Luther King and his fellow civil rights' leaders led a march on Washington, D.C., on August 28. The peaceable and orderly mass, from all walks of life and racial groups, passed the U.S. capital's great monuments to justice and liberty, and gathered in front of the most significant of all, the Lincoln Memorial. There, King "subpoenaed the conscience of the nation before the judgment seat of morality."

In his great address he said: "I have a dream that one day this nation will rise up and live out the true meaning of its creed: 'We hold these truths to be self-evident, that all men are created equal'... I have a dream that my four little children will one day live in a nation where they will not be judged by the color of their skin but by the content of their character. I have a dream today...."

"I have a dream that one day every valley shall be exalted, every hill and mountain shall be made low, the rough places will be plains, and the crooked places will be made straight, and the glory of the Lord shall be revealed, and all flesh shall see it together.

"This is our hope. This is the faith with which I shall return to the South.... With this faith we will be able to work together, to pray together, to struggle together, to go to jail together, to stand up for freedom together, knowing that we will be free one day....."

By this time, President Kennedy was already discussing the projected Civil Rights Act with his brother Robert, the attorney-general, and a wide selection of black and white leaders. Kennedy feared that the march might evoke a backlash against the legislation, and organized a specially established United Civil Rights Leadership Council to control the demonstration. In the event all went well, and the Act was passed in 1964, the same year as King was awarded the Nobel Peace Prize.

But time was running out for Martin Luther King. On April 4, 1968, he was shot dead as he stood on the balcony of the Lorraine Hotel in Memphis, Tennessee. The assassination sparked riots in more than 60 American cities. A white drifter, James Earl Ray, later confessed to the murder.

At the conclusion of his most famous speech, the Reverend Dr. Martin Luther King waves to a crowd of more than 200,000 people in the Mall in Washington, D.C.

The Profumo Affair

During the 1950s and early 1960s, Britain was plagued by a succession of spy scandals, as government officials and others were caught supplying sensitive information to the Soviet Union. But it was the relatively innocent indiscretions of war minister John Profumo that helped bring down the British Conservative government, after 13 years in office, in 1964.

Profumo first met London osteopath Stephen Ward—and his entourage of good-looking girls—in July 1961. He was staying at Cliveden, Lord Astor's huge country house perched high above the Thames valley, where Ward had a rented bungalow in the grounds. One evening, Profumo wandered down to the swimming pool, and was there confronted by Christine Keeler—stark naked.

Within days the minister was embroiled in an affair with her; but meanwhile, unknown to him, her favors were also being enjoyed by an attaché at the Soviet Embassy, Captain Eugene Ivanov. Discovering that both Profumo and Ivanov were, at different times, visitors to Ward's mews flat, British intelligence service MI5 warned the minister that the Russian was a suspected spy. Profumo then broke off his relationship with Keeler.

However, on March 21, 1963, a reference to Profumo's involvement with Keeler—and, by implication, with Ivanov—was made in parliament by Labor party politician George Wigg. On the following day Profumo read a statement to the House of Commons in which he denied any sexual relation with Christine Keeler, and added: "I shall not hesitate to issue writs for libel and slander if scandalous allegations are made or repeated outside the House."

That was enough to set loose the hounds of the press, who already knew more than they dared print. Profumo confessed his indiscretion to his wife, and then resigned. Prime minister Harold Macmillan announced his own resignation in October, and in the general election the following year the Conservatives lost to Labor. On July 22, 1963, Stephen Ward stood trial at the Old Bailey on the charge of living off immoral earnings. After eight days, when it became clear that a guilty verdict was likely, he committed suicide.

Press photographers mob Christine Keeler during her trial for perjury and obstruction of justice during the Profumo affair. She was later sentenced to nine months' imprisonment.

J.F.K. Assassination

At 12.30 pm on November 22, 1963, the Presidential motorcade entered Dealey Plaza in Dallas, Texas. Suddenly there came the sound of rifle shots. The open Lincoln convertible, carrying U.S. President John F. Kennedy and his wife Jacqueline, together with Texas Governor John Connally and his wife, swerved, then accelerated forward, followed by its speeding motorcycle escort. The President, who had been hit twice, lay across the back seat, his head cradled in his wife's lap; Connally, similarly stricken, was slumped in front. While Secret Service agents milled around in bewilderment, the limousine raced to Parkland Memorial Hospital; half an hour later Kennedy was pronounced dead—although Connally recovered in due course.

Within two hours, Dallas police had arrested Lee Harvey Oswald, a 24-year-old employee at the Texas Book Depository, who had apparently fired the shots from a window on the fifth floor of the building. Two days later, as Oswald was being transferred from the city jail to the county jail, local nightclub owner Jack Ruby, in front of television cameras, stepped forward and shot him in the stomach. Oswald died almost immediately.

The near-panic that followed the shooting—the forcible removal of Kennedy's body from Parkland Hospital to Bethesda Naval Hospital in Washington, D.C.; the secrecy surrounding the autopsy; and Oswald's bizarre death—fueled numerous conspiracy theories. The C.I.A., the Mafia, Cuban exiles: all were implicated at some stage. Oswald had lived in the Soviet Union, and it was rumored that it was not he who had killed the President, but a Soviet agent who had been substituted for him. It required an exhumation to prove that the body was indeed that of Oswald.

How many shots were fired? The Warren Report of 1964 did little to dispel rumors that Kennedy had been hit not twice but three times, and that the last shot had been fired from a different location. It was not until 1977 that forensic pathologists showed that the bullet that struck Kennedy's back had passed right through his body, and then through Connally's. A second bullet pierced the President's skull. Both bullets had been recovered. So there was no third, missing, bullet.

This snapshot was taken so soon after the assassin's first bullet found its mark that neither the accompanying police outriders nor the bystanders have yet realized what has happened.

Lakonia

It is an old sailor's superstition that changing the name of a ship brings bad luck. The superstition was certainly justified in the case of the Dutch cruise ship *Johan van Oldenbarnevelt*, which, after many voyages from Europe to America and the Antipodes, was sold to the Greek Line in 1963 and renamed *Lakonia*.

An enthusiastic brochure issued by the new owners promised that a cruise aboard *Lakonia* would be a holiday to be remembered "for the rest of your life," and for most of 1963 this proved true for many happy holidaymakers. Yet—ironically and tragically—it also proved true for those who embarked on the ship's last voyage from Southampton on December 19, 1963.

Three days later, in the evening, when the ship was in the Atlantic Ocean some 200 miles north-northeast of the Portuguese island of Madeira, fire broke out in the hairdressing salon. Two stewards attempted vainly to tackle the blaze with small extinguishers, and it was only when it was clearly out of their control that Captain Mathios Zarbis was informed. He ordered the passengers to assemble in the ship's dining saloon—this caused consternation, for the saloon was three decks down, close to the seat of the fire. Fortunately, few passengers obeyed the command.

Finally, at midnight, Zarbis ordered the lifeboats to be lowered. But the boat davits had been neglected, and were not all in working order, and in the ensuing panic only some lifeboats got away, to be picked up by four ships that had raced to the rescue. Left on board were 95 passengers and 33 crew members, who were burned to death or drowned.

The smoldering hulk was taken in tow by salvagers, but on December 29 *Lakonia* sank in 1,250 fathoms, 250 miles southwest of Gibraltar—strangely enough, close to where her sister ship, the *Marnix van St. Aldegonde,* had been torpedoed and sunk during World War II. At the subsequent inquiry into the tragedy, many of the 900 survivors gave a tribunal in Athens, Greece, shocking evidence of inadequate safety equipment and lax emergency procedures aboard the doomed *Lakonia*. The enquiry placed the blame for the disaster on lack of organization, and poor leadership by Captain Zarbis and his officers.

The Greek cruise liner Lakonia *burns out of control in the Atlantic, just before Christmas 1963. The aircraft from which this snapshot was taken could not help those left on board.*

Anti-U.S. Riots in Panama

In January 1964, in Panama City, Panama, a squad of soldiers faced a crowd of students and political activists in front of the National Legislature building. The demonstrators were calling for the Panamanian government to take a stronger line against the United States over the Panama Canal. The cry was "Yankee go home."

The United States has long taken an interest in the strategic importance of the isthmus of Panama: here, little more than 50 miles separate the waters of the Caribbean from the Pacific, offering a relatively rapid means of communication between the eastern and western American seaboards. The 1849 Californian Gold Rush was the impetus for the construction of a railroad across the isthmus, but early attempts to build a canal failed. However, within three days of Panama's declaration of independence from Colombia in 1903, the United States signed a treaty with the new nation that authorized the construction of a canal large enough to permit the passage of American warships. To protect it, the Canal Zone, a strip of land approximately 5 miles wide on each side of the canal, became U.S. territory in 1912.

Problems soon arose when Panamanian workers began agitating for pay equal to that of U.S. workers, a demand that was not met until 1958. In 1958, and again in 1959, groups of Panamanian nationalists invaded the Zone, intent on raising their own flag there. Although the United States granted this concession, the question of the flag remained highly emotional. On January 9, 1964, a dispute about the flag blew up between American and Panamanian students at Balboa High School. This led to a rapid deterioration of relations between the two countries, and furious anti-American mobs stormed the Zone.

The U.S. embassy in Panama was evacuated, and American residents of Panama moved into the Zone for safety. Many people were killed, and U.S. installations were badly damaged. Diplomatic relations were restored in April 1963, but negotiations to abrogate the 1903 treaty dragged on for years. Finally, in 1977, President Jimmy Carter obtained Congressional approval for an agreement to hand over total control of the Zone to Panama, while assuring the perpetual international neutrality of the Canal. The formal handover eventually took place on January 1, 2000.

The demonstration seems peaceful, but this was just the lull before the storm—rioting broke out shortly afterward and the soldiers charged the crowd.

Pope Visits Holy Land

In January 1964, Pope Paul VI stood on the banks of the River Jordan as he became the first Roman Catholic pontiff to set foot in the Holy Land since his original predecessor, Saint Peter.

Paul VI had been elected pope the previous summer. The Vatican was in a period of great change, much of which had been prompted by his immediate predecessor: John XXIII enjoyed contact with people, and made frequent short visits in Italy at a time when it was almost unknown for the pontiff to leave the confines of the Vatican. However, Pope John was 77 at the time of his election in 1958, and died in June 1963. There was much work—and much traveling—still to be done.

Paul VI continued John XXIII's policies. He expressed a deep interest in reconciliation with other faiths, encouraging the Roman church to cooperate with the burgeoning Ecumenical Movement; he personally met twice with the patriarch of the Greek Orthodox church, and made fruitful contact with Anglican leaders. During his reign he visited Bombay, India, in December 1964, the United Nations in New York in October 1965, and Bogotá, Colombia, in August 1968. The highlight of his travels, however, was undoubtedly this historic trip to Israel, a three-day visit to Bethlehem, Nazareth, and Jerusalem that evoked wide popular enthusiasm. At Lake Tiberias, he was mobbed by journalists and photographers as he ventured to bathe his face in the waters where Jesus Christ had told Saint Peter: "On this rock I shall build my church."

On the Way of the Cross in Jerusalem, crowds surged forward to try and touch the Pope. "I shall be crushed to death," he exclaimed, and took shelter in the chapel of the Little Sisters of Jesus. "Your Holiness," enquired the only photographer allowed into the sanctuary, "may I take photos?" "Certainly, my son, yours is a difficult profession." "And yours, also, Your Holiness," came the photographer's reply.

Later in 1964, the Pope signed an agreement with Tunisia authorizing the transfer of property that had previously been owned by the Roman Catholic church. It was the first ever agreement between the Vatican and an Islamic state. Pope Paul VI died in August 1978 at the age of 80.

Pope Paul VI announces a new era in the most dramatic possible way—by revisiting the spot on which Saint John baptized the young Jesus Christ.

Beatlemania, U.S.A.

After "Love Me Do," The Beatles' first single, made the British Top 20 in December 1962, the group's rise to stardom was fast and irresistible. The follow-up, "Please Please Me," reached Number 1 in March 1963. When "I Want to Hold Your Hand" unexpectedly took top spot in the American hit parade in January 1964, there was no question about it: The Beatles had to go to the United States. On February 7, 1964, "the lovable moptops" took off from London, England.

"It is now 6.30 a.m., Beatle time. They left London 30 minutes ago. They're out over the Atlantic Ocean, headed for New York. The temperature is 32 Beatle degrees." The early-morning disc jockey on radio station W.M.C.A. was the first to signal the coming madness. The PanAm jet carrying The Beatles touched down around midday at the recently renamed Kennedy Airport. They had been seen off from Heathrow by a thousand banner-waving fans, but this was nothing to the welcome they received in New York. Screaming, up to 15,000 girls hung from balconies, and fought with a 100-man police cordon. In the terminal building, 200 journalists awaited the group. Outside—and even inside—Manhattan's Plaza Hotel, where The Beatles were to stay, chaos reigned.

On February 9, The Beatles appeared on television on *The Ed Sullivan Show*, which was watched by 73 million Americans. The group then traveled to Washington, D.C., for their first U.S. concert before a packed audience of 5,000. Then on to Miami, Florida, where they were met by four "bathing beauties," and 7,000 screaming teenagers. Plans were quickly made for a return visit to the United States. In August, after touring Scandinavia, Holland, the Far East, and Australia, they arrived in San Francisco, California. Then it was on to 23 different cities—a journey totaling 22,441 miles. By December 1964, The Beatles, with "I Feel Fine," had topped the U.S. Hot 100 six times. This was the high-water mark of Beatlemania, a phenomenon that swept the Western world.

On August 15, 1965, they returned to New York, where they gave their greatest American concert. The capacity crowd of 55,000 fans that packed Shea Stadium made up what was, at the time, the largest-ever audience for an outdoor concert.

The Beatles arriving at Kennedy International Airport, New York. From left to right: John Lennon, Ringo Starr, Paul McCartney, and George Harrison.

Clay Wins World Title

Few had expected 22-year-old Olympic gold medallist Cassius Clay to beat the bigger, heavier—and meaner—Sonny Liston in his challenge fight in Miami, Florida, on February 25, 1964. Light-footedly dancing about the ring to avoid Liston's punches, Clay knocked out the reigning champion with a winning blow so swift that many fans failed to see it. "I don't have to be told who you want me to be," he later told reporters, "I'm free to be who I want."

Born 1942 in Louisville, Kentucky, the baby-faced Clay—"I'm pretty," he liked to boast—had already won many admirers with his wit and unashamed public arrogance. "Float like a butterfly, sting like a bee; his hands can't hit what his eyes can't see," he was to prophesy in what became his trademark mode of communication—rhymed couplets.

Soon after his triumphant bout, Clay announced his conversion to the Nation of Islam, changing his name to Muhammad Ali, and embarking on a career that made his one of the most famous—and strikingly uninjured—faces in the world. In addition, he became both a spokesman and a role model for black people.

In London, England, in 1966—"light and hard and ready to rumble," as he put it—he conclusively defeated reigning British heavyweight champion Henry Cooper. In 1967, however, Ali refused to be drafted into the U.S. Army, a move that caused him to be stripped of his world title. Three years later, his appeal against this decision was accepted by the U.S. Supreme Court, but it was not until 1974 that he regained his title, against new champion George Foreman in the "Rumble in the Jungle" held at Kinshasa, Zaire.

In this fight, Ali adopted a new tactic. Instead of his famous technique of dancing out of reach, Ali played "rope-a-dope," accepting punches until Foreman was nearly exhausted, and then springing from the ropes to k.o. his adversary. Sadly, this successful method was very likely a contributory factor to the crippling Parkinson's disease that later slowed Ali's lightning moves—and, eventually, even his speech. The fighter who had declared "I am the greatest" was reduced to a shambling figure, albeit still handsome, who struggled painfully to express himself.

"Eat your words!" exclaimed the new world heavyweight champion, Cassius Clay, as he strode across the ring to confront the boxing press.

Mods and Rockers

A strange dichotomy emerged among the young fans of popular music in Britain in 1963. There was no real logic behind it, but it was revealed in differences in the music favored, and in styles of dancing in the clubs. It soon became apparent on the streets in the distinctive way that the two groups dressed.

The first sartorial development, following the abolition of clothes rationing in the 1950s, had been the "Teds"—working-class young men who favored a studied style derived from Edwardian fashions. As time went on, this evolved into an Italianate style: sharp, narrow-cut suits, tailor-made shirts and winkle-picker shoes—it was modern, and those who adopted it began to think of themselves as "mods."

In the light of subsequent events, it is ironic that The Beatles' manager Brian Epstein should have dressed his emerging protégés in something very close to this style. For in 1963 the mods decided that The Beatles were already passé, and began to turn their attention to black music—blue beat, soul, and ska. At the other extreme were the "rockers," those who still danced to rock 'n' roll and the twist. Increasingly, the rockers became identified with that archetypally conservative group, the leather-clad motorcyclists. As if to underline the difference still further, the mods decided to favor sleek Italian mopeds, Vespas and Lambrettas.

Both groups had a tradition of violence, and confrontation was perhaps inevitable. Over the Easter holiday weekend in May 1964, fleets of motorcycles and mopeds converged on English seaside resorts such as Brighton, Hastings, and Margate, and there were much-publicized clashes on the beaches. Said one 18-year-old mod: "It was a laugh, I haven't enjoyed myself so much in a long time. It was great—the beach was like a battlefield."

The police reacted with excessive force, and some of those they arrested were later given long prison sentences. The British authorities had completely misunderstood the situation: one magistrate even described the mods, with their short haircuts and neat suits, as "long-haired beatniks." The dispute soon fizzled out naturally, the mods winning the acceptance of the fashion world, and the rockers retiring to shabby clubs where they could still dance to rock 'n' roll.

Under the concerned and watchful eye of a police constable, a gang of mods rides along the seafront at Hastings, southern England, in Spring 1964.

The Aswan Dam

Among the greatest glories of Ancient Egypt were the three temples built by Ramses II in about 1250 B.C., on the west bank of the River Nile at Abu Simbel. The principal temple has been described as the greatest rock-hewn monument in the world. The entrance façade was set back into the hillside, flanked by four huge seated statues of the pharaoh, each some 65 feet high. Smaller figures were of Ramses' queen Nefertari and their sons and daughters. The interior of the temple was a series of halls penetrating 185 feet into the rock, and decorated with colored sculpture. A second temple had six statues of Ramses and his queen 33 feet high on the façade, while the third was a single rock-hewn chamber.

For years it was feared that these beautiful sculptures would have to be sacrificed to help Egypt's economic progress, but they were saved thanks to a unique program of international aid and cooperation.

The water of the Nile is essential for Egyptian agriculture, but its floods could be devastating, and in 1902 a dam was built above the town of Aswan. It was twice heightened, raising the water level upstream nearly 120 feet in late autumn, and flooding the beautiful temple of Isis on the island of Philae. In the 1950s, the proposal to build an even higher dam, 4 miles further upstream, was announced. Archaeologists realized that Abu Simbel would be completely submerged, and in 1955 an international team set to work to record the site in detail. The Egyptian government appealed to U.N.E.S.C.O. for help, and in 1960, as work began on the dam, an operation was launched to relocate some 20 temples and shrines.

Not only the giant statues at Abu Simbel, but also the temple interiors, were cut into blocks, and lifted 200 feet above the original site, where they were reassembled on the plateau, then covered once more by artificial hills to reproduce the appearance of the original landscape. The major part of this massive work was concluded in late 1967. In gratitude for a U.S. contribution of $16 million, the Egyptian government presented the United States with another temple, that of Dendur, which was shipped to the Metropolitan Museum of Art in New York. The High Dam at Aswan became operational in 1970.

Press photographers record the moment as bulldozers begin the colossal task of moving the historic monuments at Abu Simbel above the waters of the soon to be opened Aswan Dam.

Topless Fashion

For centuries, the purpose of fashion—particularly women's fashion—has been to accentuate the sexual attractions of the human body. But in the 1960s, while the leading Paris fashion houses continued to dress their models in boned and wired bras, and tightly constricting girdles, a very different influence was infiltrating from the streets and from subversive British and American designers. Young women, with their newly gained sexual freedom, also wanted freedom of movement: and that meant short skirts, softly clinging dresses, jeans, and as little as possible in the way of restricting undergarments.

The most revolutionary of the American designers was Rudi Gernreich. He was born in Vienna in 1922, and escaped from the Nazis to Los Angeles in 1938. For six years he was a professional dancer but, admitting his limited talent, he took up fashion design. His dance experience persuaded him that movement must be unencumbered, and that attempts to change the shape of a woman's body only obscured its natural beauty. It was with this in mind that he designed the "no-bra bra"— as far from the stitched and boned creations of the time as it was possible to go. This gently-supporting garment went well with the slim styles that were coming in, and it was enthusiastically adopted—although many well-endowed women were heard to mutter bitterly that it was "the no-bra bra for the no-bust bust."

Gernreich took the principle even further, and his most sensational design was the topless swimsuit introduced in 1964. Soon topless dresses—leaving the breasts exposed, or at most lightly covered with a revealing no-bra bra—were to be found on sale in even the most conventional shops. How many were actually sold, and worn, even in private, is, however, open to question. In London, three young women who dared to appear in public in this scandalous fashion were arrested and fined at Bow Street magistrates' court for "creating a public nuisance."

In the form designed by Gernreich the topless swimsuit never caught on, but the publicity it attracted contributed greatly to the ambience of the decade. Although designs such as this quickly vanished, they left their mark—today there is scarcely a public beach in the Western world where women do not sunbathe topless.

Against a backdrop of the Golden Gate Bridge, San Francisco, a model parades the latest fashion of 1964—a topless woollen bathing suit.

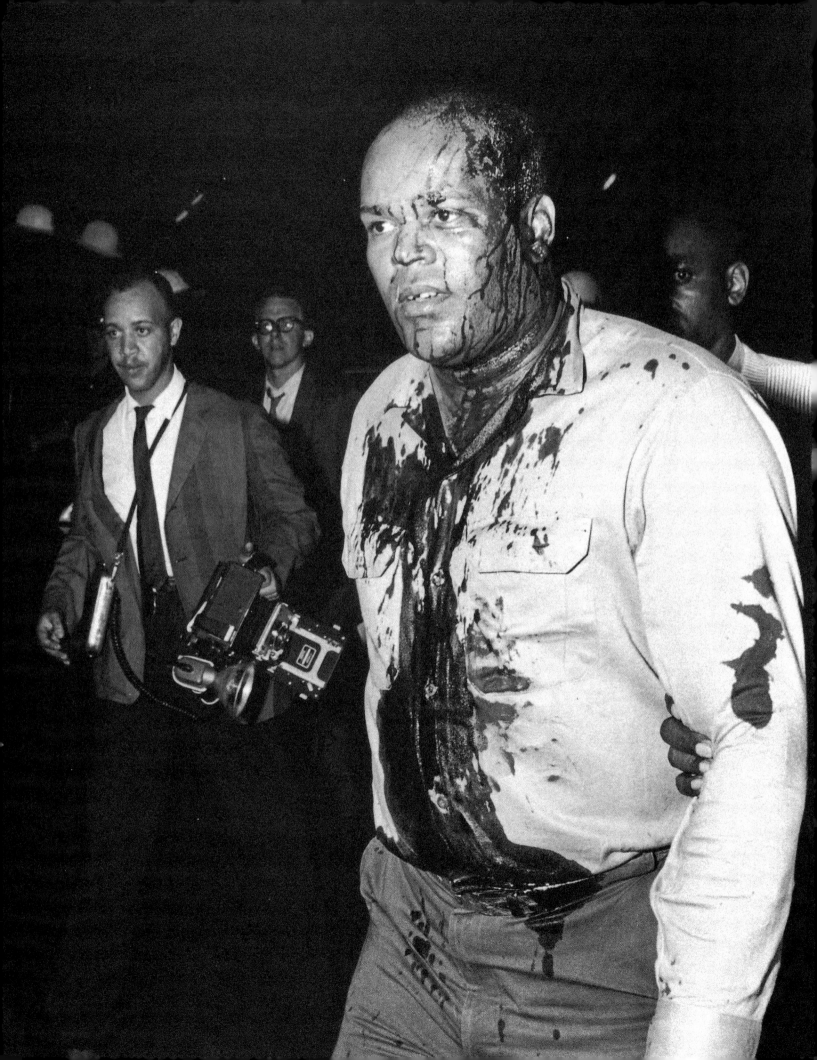

Summer Race Riots

In July 1964 a white, off-duty policeman shot and killed a 15-year-old black teenager, James Powell, in Harlem, New York City. The slaying naturally brought protests, but at first they were peaceful. Then, on the third day, the crowds that had gathered outside the local police station grew violent. They hurled rocks, bricks, and bottles, set garbage bins on fire, and looted stores, including those selling guns.

Addressing the rioters through a loudhailer, a police officer told them : "Go home! Go home!" And a voice from the crowd replied: "We are home, baby!" The rioting lasted five days, spreading to the district of Bedford-Stuyvesant. One person was killed, and 520 were arrested.

U.S. civil rights campaigners, led by the Chicago-based Student Nonviolent Coordinating Committee (S.N.C.C.), had previously declared that the summer of 1964 would be "Freedom Summer." But the threat of violence spread through many parts of the country—it was not just Harlem that was affected. In October, two black people were killed in the bombing of a church in Vicksburg, Mississippi, that was being used as a voter registration center.

Then three S.N.C.C. volunteers—two white students and a black Mississippian—who had arrived in Mississippi in June to help register black voters, disappeared one night, after being stopped in their car for alleged speeding. Their battered, bullet-ridden bodies were discovered six weeks later in a newly erected mud dam. Several Ku Klux Klan members—including the local sheriff—were eventually arrested and convicted of the murders.

Racial tension remained high in many parts of the United States; even landmark civil rights legislation did little to reduce it. On August 11, 1965, less than a week after the Voting Rights Act had been passed into law, the mainly black inhabitants of Watts, a slum district of Los Angeles, began rioting and looting after a young man was beaten up by police. It took 20,000 National Guardsmen five days to restore order; in the intervening period, 34 people died, and damage to property in the suburb was estimated at $40 million. These events were a great blow to the hopes of liberal America; the civil rights' movement began to fragment.

A wounded man walks away from the riots that were sparked off after July 16, 1964. The violence engulfed peaceable residents, shopkeepers, and passers-by.

Verrazano-Narrows Bridge

The Verrazano-Narrows Bridge, built in 1964, was the first direct road link between Brooklyn and Staten Island, New Jersey—all existing routes between the two boroughs went over bridges or through tunnels across downtown Manhattan, contributing greatly to congestion.

The bridge stands at the southern end of New York harbor. With a single main span of 4,260 feet, it was the longest suspension bridge in the world at that time, and was not exceeded in length until the Humber Bridge in England, at 4,582 feet, was opened in 1981. The current record is held by Japan's Akashi Kaikyo Bridge, opened in 1998, an impressive 6,500-feet span.

The two massive towers from which the Verrazano-Narrows Bridge is suspended rise 690 feet above the water, and stand on foundations sunk to depths of up to 170 feet. Because the towers are built perpendicular to the Earth's curved surface, they are just over an inch further apart at the top than at the base. The four main suspension cables that pass over the top of the towers are each 35 inches in diameter, and weigh nearly 10,000 tons apiece. The roadway—two decks, one above the other, each carrying a six-lane highway—weighs a further 60,000 tons. The total weight of steel in the bridge is 150,000 tons. During the heat of summer, because of the expansion of the steel cables, the roadways hang nearly 12 feet lower than in the winter. The overall cost of the bridge was $325 million.

The Verrazano-Narrows Bridge was designed by the Swiss-born engineer Othmar Hermann Ammann, who died at the age of 86 in the year following its opening. He was also responsible for the Lincoln Tunnel under the Hudson River, Dulles International Airport in Washington, D.C., and New York City's Lincoln Center for the Performing Arts, as well as the George Washington Bridge in New York (a 3,500-feet span), and San Francisco's Golden Gate Bridge (4,200 feet).

Viewed from Manhattan, the Verrazano-Narrows Bridge is an elegant structure that encloses the distant horizon; it is also the first landmark for ships approaching New York from the Atlantic Ocean. However, the bridge scarcely relieved road congestion, for its opening sparked a 30-year building boom on Staten Island!

An aerial view of the Verrazano-Narrows Bridge in November 1964, after its completion but shortly before it was opened to road traffic.

The Death of Churchill

"This was the last time that such a thing could happen," wrote Patrick O'Donovan in the British Sunday newspaper *The Observer*. "This was the last time that London would be the capital of the world. This was an act of mourning for the Imperial past. This marked the final act of Britain's greatness."

Sir Winston Churchill—Nobel laureate, painter, statesman, warrior, writer, and the man popularly credited with having led Britain to victory in World War II—had been prime minister from 1940 to 1945, and again from 1951 to 1955, when he resigned because of ill health. By then he was 81 years old, and his declining mental state had been discreetly concealed from the public for some time. Still he remained a parliamentary backbencher, and in his last years he was frequently described as "the greatest living Englishman." He died, aged 90, on January 24, 1965, and was buried six days later.

Churchill's career had not been without low points—he was responsible for the disastrous Gallipoli campaign in 1915 during World War I, and lived through "wilderness years" during which he was denied political advancement. But, for one day at least in January 1965, his failings and disappointments were forgotten. Dwight D. Eisenhower said: "Churchill was Britain—the embodiment of British defiance to threat, her courage in adversity, her calmness in danger, her moderation in success."

Churchill was the first British commoner to be honored with a state funeral since the Duke of Wellington in 1852. His body was borne in an oak coffin covered with the Union flag on a huge gun carriage, hauled by a team of servicemen, through the streets of London, from the Palace of Westminster to the steps of St. Paul's Cathedral. There it was carried in by eight red-coated guardsmen, followed by officers bearing trays of Churchill's medals, and by generals and heads of state from all over the world.

After the solemn funeral service, Churchill's coffin was taken up the River Thames on a ceremonial barge, while pipers skirled and dockside gantries dipped in farewell salute, thence transferred to the train. He was buried in a simple village churchyard near his family's ancestral home at Blenheim Palace, in Oxfordshire.

January 30, 1965: The body of Sir Winston Churchill is loaded onto a train at London Waterloo station on the journey to its final resting place in Bladon, Oxfordshire.

Bombing Vietnam

From 1965, the conflict in Vietnam became a U.S. war, but the Southeast Asian nation had not always been an American concern. Between 1893 and 1954, Vietnam, together with Cambodia and Laos, had been known collectively as Indochina, which was part of the French Empire. However, after the defeat of France by Germany in 1940, and the conquest of Indochina by Japan in the following year, a nationalist movement developed in northern Vietnam—the Viet Minh, led by a Communist, Ho Chi Minh.

On September 2, 1945, the Democratic Republic of Vietnam was declared in Hanoi, but French forces soon reoccupied Indochina. A protracted guerrilla war ensued, and continued until the French admitted defeat after the loss of their stronghold at Dien Bien Phu in 1954. The Geneva Accords signed in that year recognized the independence of Laos and Cambodia, and divided Vietnam into a northern communist state, with its capital Hanoi, and a southern state with its capital Saigon. However, there were still many pockets of Viet Minh in the south, and North Vietnam initiated a new guerrilla war against the partitioned territory.

The Americans built up the South Vietnamese army with tanks and artillery, but these were totally unsuited to fighting guerrillas. President Kennedy was deeply alarmed by developments, and in December 1961 two helicopter companies of American "military advisers" were sent to Saigon. By 1964, the Viet Minh—now known as the Viet Cong—were clearly winning on the ground, and in August of that year they attacked U.S. ships in the Gulf of Tonkin. The new American president, Lyndon Johnson, was given extensive military powers in Vietnam by Congress, and by December there were 23,000 U.S. troops in the country.

On February 5, 1965, the Viet Cong attacked U.S. bases in South Vietnam. Two days later, U.S. President Lyndon Johnson ordered operation "Rolling Thunder." The U.S. Air Force began bombing supply lines, dumps, and oil installations in North Vietnam. These were supposed to be limited strikes against key targets, but there was soon further escalation, with U.S. ground forces attacking isolated villages and plantations suspected of harboring the Viet Cong.

As the Vietnam War escalates, a U.S. munitions factory worker sends a personal message to the enemy. This bomb was one of the first to be dropped in a long and ineffective campaign.

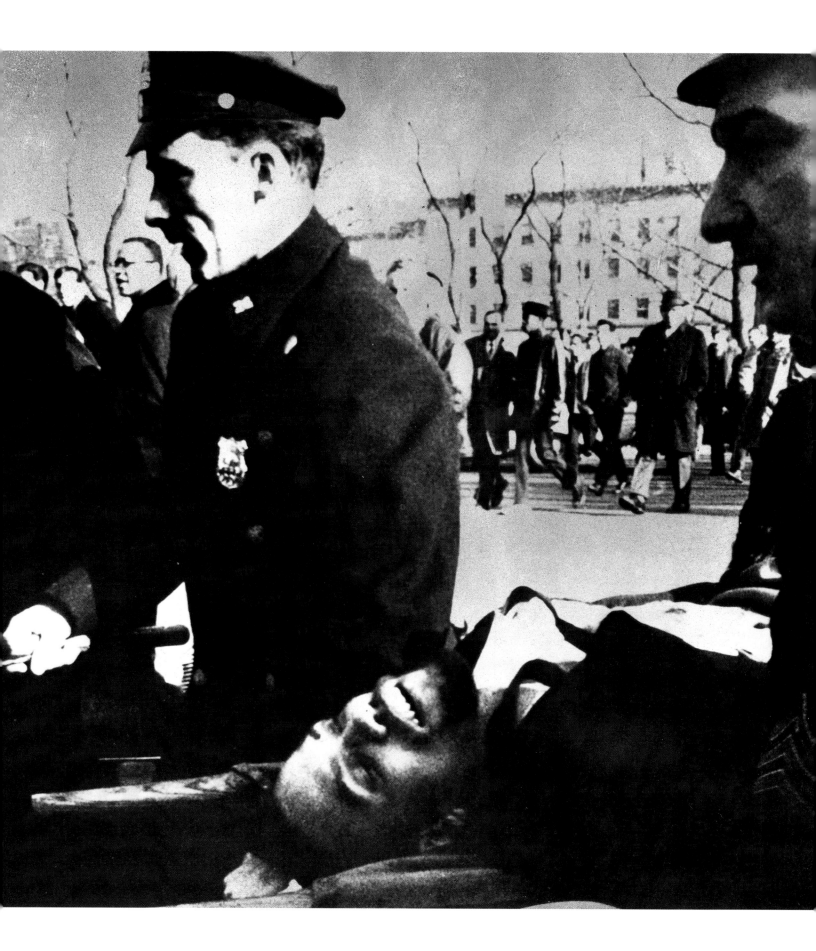

Malcolm X Assassinated

Born in 1925, in 1931 Malcolm Little saw his father, a Baptist minister, murdered, and his home burned by white racists. Arrested for burglary in Boston, Massachusetts, in 1946, and imprisoned for seven years, Little came under the influence of Elijah Muhammad, the leader of the Nation of Islam, otherwise known as the Black Muslims. This was a nationalist sect that regarded whites as "devils," and hoped to establish a separate black state. On his release in 1952, Little took the name Malcolm X to replace the surname that had been given to his family by slave owners, and adopted the rigid code of discipline imposed by the Black Muslims: dark suits, white shirts, close-cropped hair, and abstemious ways.

With his fine speaking voice, Malcolm X soon became the leading advocate for the Nation of Islam, and Elijah Muhammad gave him the task of setting up mosques in, among other places, Detroit, Michigan, and Harlem, New York. Malcolm X was credited with increasing membership of the Black Muslims from 500 to 30,000 over the following 10 years.

Malcolm X preached rejection of all white values, opposing the integrationist, nonviolent principles of Martin Luther King, Jr. Increasingly, he clashed with Elijah Muhammad on doctrinal matters, and split from the Nation of Islam in 1964, founding the Muslim Mosque, Inc. In the same year, he made a pilgrimage to Mecca, Saudi Arabia, where he found Muslims of all races worshiping together, including "blond-haired, blue-eyed men I could call my brothers." On his return to the United States, he founded the Organization of Afro-American Unity.

Relations with the conservative Elijah Muhammad were now fraught, and Malcolm X was warned that he had been marked for assassination. He began to travel everywhere with bodyguards, but when the time came they were unable to save him. His killers, all three members of the Nation of Islam, were convicted of first-degree murder in March 1966. Despite his reputation as an extremist, *The Autobiography of Malcolm X*, transcribed by Alex Haley, the author of *Roots*, and published shortly after Malcolm's death, holds out a slim hope of social justice, and reconciliation between blacks and whites.

On February 21, 1965, the body of Malcolm X is removed from the Audubon Ballroom in Manhattan, New York, where he was speaking when he was shot 15 times at close range.

First U.S. Space Walk

By 1965, the "race for the Moon" initiated by President Kennedy was hotting up. Among the many remarkable technical developments in this period, one in particular required essential practical investigation. The main question was: could a man survive outside the space capsule if he was wearing a pressurized suit? And if so, could he perform useful activities while out there?

The Americans thought their research was well advanced, but to their chagrin, the Soviet Union found the answer first. On March 18, high above Siberia, cosmonaut Aleksei Leonov took a 10-minute walk in space outside Voshkod 2.

Yet although the Russians won that stage of the race to the Moon, their operation received much less acclaim than the first American extravehicular activity (E.V.A.), not least because, unlike Voshkod, the whole Gemini 4 mission was watched by the world's television and news media.

The American spacecraft was launched into orbit from Cape Kennedy on June 3. When it reached its cruising altitude of 200 miles above the surface of the Earth, and a speed of around 18,000 m.p.h., astronaut Ed White stepped outside. He remained tethered to the spacecraft by a 25-feet-long umbilical hose that provided oxygen and contained wiring through which he communicated with his fellow astronaut, Jim McDivitt, who remained on board to pilot the vessel. In his left hand White clutched a hand-held self-maneuvering unit (H.H.S.M.U.), a twin-barreled gun that shot short bursts of nitrogen gas, which enabled him to change position at will.

White remained outside in space for 22 minutes, traveling 5,000 miles over the Indian and Pacific Oceans. After 62 orbits, Gemini splashed down in the Atlantic.

On their return to Earth, both astronauts were promoted to the rank of lieutenant colonel. In addition, they received several civic awards, and were awarded honorary doctorates by the University of Michigan. Joked White: "I can hardly get used to people calling me 'colonel.' I know in a million years I'll never get used to people calling me 'doctor'."

Ed White died in a fire during a test exercise aboard Apollo 1 in January 1967, along with fellow astronauts Roger Chaffee and Gus Grissom.

On June 3, 1965, astronaut Edward H. White II, a former U.S. Air Force test pilot, becomes the first American to walk in space during the Gemini 4 four-day Earth orbital mission.

Mary Quant's Miniskirt

Although the miniskirt hit the headlines in 1965, its earliest origins can be traced back to 1957, when British fashion designer Mary Quant, then aged 24, and her husband Alexander Plunkett-Green opened a boutique named Bazaar on the King's Road in Chelsea, London, England, where she sold clothes designed—and frequently made—by herself. Nearby was the Chelsea School of Art, where some female students were already beginning to wear skirts that finished above the knee.

The word "mini" really caught the popular imagination in 1959 with the launch of the revolutionary Mini Minor car designed by Alec Issigonis and manufactured by Morris Motors. When Quant introduced her first "miniskirt," some 6 or 7 inches shorter than had been seen since the 1920s, its success was assured. With the miniskirt came tights, which afforded an acceptable degree of modesty. Economic considerations also played their part. Less fabric meant a more affordable price, and in Britain clothing for children—which these short skirts could plausibly claim to be—was not subject, like adult clothes, to purchase tax.

Then, in 1965, Paris designer André Courrèges launched his autumn show with a parade of girls in white boots and skirts that, while not as short as those sold in Bazaar, provoked a horrified response. "Every time I do something modern, with love and enthusiasm," complained Courrèges, "I am criticized."

Once the miniskirt had obtained the endorsement of French couturiers, it caught on all over the world, and met the expected disapproval of the older generation. In a school in Tennessee, girls were suspended for wearing skirts judged too short by the principal, who pointed out that the school had open stairways, and the fact that girls were sometimes at the top, and boys at the bottom, created "a distraction from the educational process." And in 1970 police claimed, unbelievably, that, "since the introduction of the miniskirt... rape is up 68 percent in the United States, 90 percent in England."

This shortest of short skirts has survived all the changes in fashion. And as Mary Quant has said: "It wasn't me or Courrèges who invented the miniskirt anyway... it was the girls in the street who did it."

Mary Quant, modeling her famous creation. She was one of the first in a new wave of Anglo-Saxons to challenge the supremacy of French stylists in the world of high fashion.

War Over Kashmir

The ruggedly beautiful north Indian state of Kashmir has been the cause of constant dispute between India and Pakistan since 1947. In that year, the Indian subcontinent gained independence from British rule, and was partitioned into two new nations—predominantly Hindu India in the east, and Islamic Pakistan in the west. But many problems were caused by more than 560 independent principalities. They were declared free to accede to either of the new nations, and the geographical position of most ensured that they moved into India's sphere of influence. In Junagadh, however, the Muslim nawab chose Pakistan, even though 80 percent of his subjects were Hindu—a situation that was resolved only when Indian troops occupied the state, and a plebiscite secured it for India.

Kashmir presented a more complex problem. It had common borders with both India and Pakistan—as well as with China—and, although the majority of the population was Muslim, the maharajah was a Hindu. When Pathan tribesmen invaded the state in October 1947, he appealed to India for help. Troops were sent from India, while the Pathans were reinforced by Pakistanis. Eventually, the United Nations' Security Council appointed a peacemaking commission, and India's claim to a major part of Kashmir was confirmed on January 1, 1949.

In 1959, and again in 1962, Chinese troops invaded Kashmir from the north, and in 1963 China signed an agreement with Pakistan defining a 300-mile border. Major world powers all took an interest in the continuing conflict of sovereignty. China's support of Pakistan provoked protests from the Soviet Union, which regarded India as a vital buffer against Chinese expansionism; the United States favored India for the same reason.

In August 1965, more than 5,000 Pakistani troops, disguised as civilians, crossed into Indian-held Kashmir, and fighting broke out all along the former ceasefire line. The U.N. Security Council ordered a truce, which came into force on September 23. In Tashkent in January 1966, the Soviet Union brokered a more lasting settlement between India and Pakistan. Both nations renounced the use of force in Kashmir, but even today the peace there remains uneasy.

Blindfolded and chained, Pakistani soldiers are taken for interrogation by Indian authorities after allegedly crossing the border into the disputed territory of Kashmir.

Rhodesian U.D.I.

The vast tract of southern central Africa known as Rhodesia was named after Cecil Rhodes, the British-born empire builder, who formed the British South Africa Company in 1889. In due course it was divided into two British-controlled protectorates, and in 1923 Southern Rhodesia became a self-governing colony. In 1953, the Federation of Rhodesia and Nyasaland was formed by the British government, but it was dissolved in the following year, Nyasaland becoming the independent state of Malawi, and Northern Rhodesia independent Zambia.

That left Southern Rhodesia, with its black population of four million outnumbering the white settlers by 16 to 1. The whites, however, were very much in day-to-day control. The prime minister, Ian Smith, had already begun agitating for independence from the British Commonwealth, while the installation of black governments in the other ex-Federation countries raised fears among white Rhodesians. When the British government refused to consider Smith's claims, on November 11, 1965, he announced his country's unilateral declaration of independence (U.D.I.) from Britain.

Britain immediately imposed economic sanctions, and the United Nations soon followed suit. But, as *The Guardian* newspaper said at the time: "Whether [the sanctions] will prove adequate to bring Rhodesia to its knees... must be doubtful. As an agricultural country, Rhodesia is almost self-supporting."

Yet U.D.I. did not work in the way Ian Smith and his supporters hoped. In the short term it brought a bloody civil war, a three-sided conflict between Rhodesian security forces, the Zimbabwe People's Revolutionary Army led by Joshua Nkomo, and the Zimbabwe National Liberation Army led by Robert Mugabe. This conflict dragged on until 1979, when a free democratic election installed Bishop Abel Muzorewa as the first black prime minister, and the country was renamed Zimbabwe. In a second election held in February 1980, voters were terrorized by supporters of Robert Mugabe, who then took over the country. In the view of many, the long term consequence of U.D.I. has been the subsequent decline of Zimbabwe under Mugabe into an undemocratic one-party state.

Downtown Salisbury, Southern Rhodesia (now Harare, Zimbabwe) on the day after the white minority rulers announced the country's U.D.I. from Britain.

Penn Station Demolished

Before 1966, New York City had two grandiose railroad terminals; after the demolition of Penn Station, there was only one—Grand Central Station.

> "You leave that Pennsylvania Station 'bout a quarter to four,
>
> Read a magazine, and then you're in Baltimore.
>
> Dinner in the diner, nothing could be finer,
>
> Than to have your ham and eggs in Carolina...."

The 1941 song "Chattanooga Choo-Choo" celebrated the pleasures of travel from the New York terminus of the Pennsylvania Railroad, one of the glories of the city. Before it was built, passengers from Manhattan to Philadelphia and beyond had to take the train from New Jersey, which they reached by ferry across the Hudson River; but by 1900 new electric locomotives were able to haul trains through tunnels under the river to where the huge coal-fired locos waited with steam up.

Penn Station was sited in Manhattan as a direct challenge to the dominance of the New York Central Railroad. It was designed in 1902 by leading architects McKim, Mead & White, begun three years later, and completed in 1911, and was the largest structure of modern times to be built in one stretch: it enclosed 28 acres of two city blocks. The façade was inspired by the colonnade that surrounds the piazza of St. Peter's in the Vatican City, and the immense waiting-room was based on the Baths of Caracalla in ancient Rome. It soared a vertiginous 150 feet to a coffered and vaulted ceiling, supported by 84 massive pillars, and echoed cavernously with the hubbub of hundreds of passing travelers. Branched electric lamps on tall columns illuminated the waiting-room, where, curiously, there was not a single bench on which to wait. The ramps and tracks of the train concourse beyond were covered by glass vaulting and intricate steel framing.

When plans to knock down Penn Station were announced, architectural experts protested strongly but in vain. The magnificent building was replaced by a low-lying, utilitarian terminal—"a repellent warren"—and a sports complex. Said architectural historian Professor Vincent Scully: "One entered the city like a god.... One scuttles in now like a rat."

A New York landmark for many years, the old Penn Station was demolished in January 1966 to make way for the new Madison Square Garden.

World Cup Stolen

The eighth soccer World Cup was held in England in 1966. As part of the publicity build-up, the trophy itself was displayed at a stamp exhibition held by the Stanley Gibbons Company in Central Hall, Westminster, London. Although known as a cup, the sport's top prize was then in reality a 14-inch-high gold statuette weighing 8 pounds and representing an allegorical winged victory on an octagonal base.

Sensationally, after two days on show, the cup was stolen from its case in the hall. A man was soon arrested, but there was no sign of the trophy, and the world soccer authorities had to lay hasty plans for staging a tournament without a prize.

One week later a mongrel dog named Pickles became interested in a package wrapped in newspaper that he found in a garden while being taken for a walk in Norwood, South London. His owner, David Corbett, decided to have a closer look, and discovered the missing World Cup, which had been abandoned there when thieves found it too hot to handle.

Pickles was feted, and awarded a silver medal by the National Canine Defense League. He was also given a year's supply of dog food, but sadly he did not live to enjoy it all—not long afterward he chased a cat up a tree, and hanged himself.

The final of the tournament, on July 30, was between England, the hosts, and West Germany. The game was watched by 100,000 spectators at Wembley Stadium. England conceded a goal after only 13 minutes, to the German Haller, but six minutes later, Geoff Hurst scored an equalizer. The score remained one-all until Martin Peters slammed a second goal, with only 12 minutes left to play. An England victory looked certain, but a scrambled goal by Wolfgang Weber, seconds before the final whistle, forced the match into a 30-minute period of extra time.

The goal that followed in the 100th minute has remained a controversy in soccer history. Hurst's shot hit the underside of the crossbar, rebounded down onto the line, and bounced back out. The referee was in doubt, but the linesman declared it a goal. Then, with only seconds to spare, Hurst completed his hat-trick. England had won 4–2, and a few moments later captain Bobby Moore lifted the World Cup. But without the keen nose of Pickles there might have been no trophy to receive.

March 18, 1966: A security guard hands over the soccer World Cup to the sales manager of Stanley Gibbons. Two days later, it mysteriously disappeared.

Timothy Leary

A leading advocate of the unrestricted availability and use of drugs, Dr. Timothy Leary was controversially arrested in New York on his return from Toronto, Canada, under a Federal law that prohibits users of narcotics from leaving or reentering the United States without permission.

Leary, a doctor of clinical psychology, joined the Harvard Center for Research in Personality in 1958, and two years later reported "the deepest religious experience of my life" after eating seven "sacred mushrooms." Soon afterward he helped found the *Psychedelic Review*, and became an advocate of what he termed "consciousness-expanding" drugs. Although Leary's ideas were new to some people, most of his work merely repeated experiments carried out more than a decade earlier by British writer Aldous Huxley, who described them in *The Doors of Perception* (1954).

Leary offered drugs to volunteers at Harvard, but the authorities were deeply concerned, and when Leary refused to discontinue his experiments he was asked to leave the university. He then set up the privately funded International Foundation for Internal Freedom.

"Turn on, tune in, drop out"—Leary explained this famous mantra in the following terms: "'Turn on' means to contact the ancient energies and wisdoms that are built into your nervous system.... 'Tune in' means to harness and communicate these new perspectives in a harmonious dance with the external world. 'Drop out' means to detach yourself from the tribal game."

Leary was particularly keen on LSD—lysergic acid diethylamide, which occurs naturally in the grain fungus ergot. Its psychedelic effects had not been recognized until 1943, when the Swiss chemist Albert Hofmann accidentally swallowed some that he had synthesized. Until 1966, LSD was legally available from pharmaceutical suppliers, as well as bootleg sources. Many pop musicians admitted "taking a trip," and The Beatles' song "Lucy in the Sky with Diamonds" was said to allude to its effects. But there were fears that the "mind-altered" state it induced could cause psychological damage, and numerous scare stories were publicized. In April, Sandoz Pharmaceuticals announced that they were withdrawing LSD from sale.

October 11, 1966: Dr. Timothy Leary (center) is escorted into a New York customs house after his arrest at the city's La Guardia Airport.

Stokely Carmichael

During a speech at a political rally outside the State Capitol in Jackson, Mississippi, Stokely Carmichael introduced the slogan "Black Power" to a wider audience, and thus opened a rift between himself and Martin Luther King, Jr.

Born in Trinidad in 1941, Carmichael was educated in the United States after his family moved to New York. While still a student at Howard University, Washington, D.C.—which he had chosen in preference to several white universities that had offered him scholarships—Carmichael joined the Freedom Riders of the Congress of Racial Equality, a radical human rights' organization that challenged segregated buses in the South. On graduating with a bachelor's degree in philosophy in 1964—"Freedom Summer"—he became an active member, and later chairman, of the Student Non-Violent Coordinating Committee (S.N.C.C.), which supported positive action against segregation.

Yet he soon grew dissatisfied with established parties, and so formed his own, which took as its symbol—significantly—a black panther. Tall, slim, and supremely confident, Carmichael was said to look as if he was strutting, even while standing still. *Life* magazine in 1967 described him as a man who could "stroll through Dixie in broad daylight using the Confederate flag for a handkerchief."

Carmichael's Jackson speech brewed a storm of controversy, and was denounced by black and white moderates. Martin Luther King called it "an unfortunate choice of words." Said another black leader: "Anyone can arouse the poor, the despairing, the helpless. That's no trick. Sure, they'll shout 'black power' but... how many of those people will follow those leaders to a separate state or back to Africa?"

In 1967 the S.N.C.C. severed all ties with Carmichael. He then became "prime minister" of the Black Panthers, now an ultramilitant urban organization, but he soon decided that they, too, were not sufficiently radical. He moved to Guinea in Africa, and became a globe-trotting ambassador for the All African Peoples Revolutionary Party. In 1978 he took the name of Kwame Ture, in honor of two African socialist leaders, Kwame Nkrumah of Ghana, and Ahmed Sekou Toure of Guinea. Stokely Carmichael died in Africa in November 1998.

June 16, 1966: Stokely Carmichael addresses the March Against Fear: "We have been saying 'Freedom' for six years. What we are going to start saying now is 'Black Power.'"

Twiggy

Lesley Hornby was born in 1949 in the featureless suburb of Neasden in northwest London, England. At the age of 15 she was a thin, knock-kneed schoolgirl, awkward, and inclined to chew her fingernails—but she had a pert and undeniably photogenic face. One day, she went to the salon of local hairdresser Tony Davies, and there met the proprietor's brother, an assistant to an antiques dealer. Although his name was Nigel, he called himself Justin de Villeneuve. He was stunned by her appearance: "There was this lovely little girl," he later recalled, "so tiny and so beautiful. She was breathtaking."

Tony arranged for Lesley, whom he nicknamed "Twiggy" because of her gawkiness, to be photographed. Claimed Justin: "That was the moment I knew I would crack it. I knew a few models… and Twiggy just had something about her that was absolutely right." But at only 5 feet 6 inches in height, and weighing less than 100 pounds, she was too small for the model agencies, and it was only Justin's persistence over the following months that got her taken on for head-shots in fashion photos. Then the fashion editor of *The Daily Express* newspaper spotted her, and gave her a full page, with the headline: "This is the face of '66—Twiggy, the Cockney kid with the face to launch a thousand shops, and she's only sixteen."

Happily, Twiggy's build was just right for the skimpy clothes then being sold at London boutiques such as Bazaar and Biba, and hers rapidly became, not just the face, but also the figure of 1966. Miniskirts and skinny knitted tops fitted her to perfection, and her photograph appeared in magazines everywhere "with hair bobbed, wide eyes made up in triple tiers of false eyelashes, and a figure like a beanpole." When she arrived in the United States in 1967, she was greeted at the airport by more delirious fans and scrimmaging photographers than had turned out for anyone since The Beatles in 1964.

Twiggy's career as a photographic fashion model did not last long, but in 1971 she played the lead in Ken Russell's film *The Boy Friend*. It was when Justin fell out with the director over film credits that the relationship between the model and her Svengali finally broke up.

Twiggy appeared in several more films after her split from Justin de Villeneuve. She also starred on Broadway, and made a number of records, before retiring from the public gaze.

Mao Swims

In a publicity stunt that surprised and baffled the Western world, Mao Zedong, the 73-year-old chairman of the Chinese communist party, swam in the Yangtze River. Why had the normally reticent head of a closed society done such a thing in front of the cameras?

The answer soon emerged. Mao was facing the hostility of many of his top officials, who felt that he was too old to remain in power. In April he began a purge of the party bureaucracy, and announced the launch of the Great Proletarian Cultural Revolution, which was designed to destroy "revisionism" and restore China to pure Marxism. Mao called on university students to "learn revolution by making revolution;" they responded by forming the Red Guards, a huge and violent movement dedicated to rooting out bourgeois "ghosts and monsters," and to reestablishing a largely peasant population. It has been estimated that the Cultural Revolution resulted in the deaths of 400,000 innocent people.

To quash persistent rumors that he was ailing, Mao decided on a dramatic demonstration of his good health. On the morning of July 16, a vast crowd gathered among a forest of red flags along the banks of the Yangtze in Hunan province. Accompanied by 15 Red Guards, Mao embarked in a launch that carried him to the vicinity of the Changjiang bridge. There, his huge bulk clad only in elasticated swimming trunks, he ponderously descended a ladder into the water, followed by his guards, and remained there for over an hour.

Whether Mao was truly swimming is in doubt. According to the memoirs of his personal physician, he could not swim, and was kept afloat by his vast girth. Yet photographs of the event helped confirm Mao's continuing power in China.

Following this, July 16 was declared "national swimming day." Each subsequent year, hordes of Chinese took to the water in rivers, lakes, and at sea, and swimming competitions were held throughout the country. The Chinese leader's example so impressed Deng Xiaoping, who succeeded Mao on his death in 1976, that he, too, was photographed swimming, in the same spot, on the day that he announced a radical modernization program.

To prove that rumors of his demise had been exaggerated, and that he was still a force to be reckoned with, Chairman Mao (foreground) swims in the Yangtze River on July 16, 1966.

PRIVATE EYE

No. 124
Friday
17 Sept. 66

1/6

VERWOERD

A NATION MOURNS

Verwoerd Assassinated

On September 6, 1966, Hendrik Verwoerd, prime minister of South Africa, was stabbed to death as he sat waiting for the start of a session of parliament in the government building in Cape Town. His assailant, Dimetrios Tsafendas, a white messenger, later said that he killed Verwoerd because he was too liberal.

To the outside world, this seemed an odd way of describing one of the founding fathers of apartheid. Born in Amsterdam, Netherlands, in 1901, Verwoerd had lived in South Africa since he was three months old. In 1937, he was appointed editor of a new Johannesburg daily, *Die Transvaler*, and during World War II the newspaper, under his direction, took a strongly pro-Nazi line.

Verwoerd became vice-chairman of the National Party of the Transvaal in 1946, was elected a senator in 1948, and appointed minister of native affairs in 1950. In this position he was responsible for framing the major part of the apartheid laws, designed to maintain white supremacy in South Africa.

In the election of 1958 Verwoerd won a seat in the South African House of Assembly. When the leader of the Nationalist Party, Johannes Strijdom, died soon after, Verwoerd became the new leader of the party, and took office as prime minister the following day. He then worked hard to remove South Africa from the British Commonwealth, and to establish an independent republic. In October 1960, a national referendum approved this move by a narrow margin. In 1963, Verwoerd authorized the arrest and detention of Nelson Mandela.

The photograph shows how the apartheid politician's death was viewed by the British fortnightly *Private Eye*. Founded in the fall of 1961, the magazine was full of topical comments, cartoons, jokes, and photographs with speech bubbles. The publication soon started to print stories that the mainstream press dared not run, for fear of libel actions. Many of those who were written about said the pieces were scurrilous, but much of what appeared in *Private Eye* at the time turned out to be true. Thus, despite its rather low-grade production quality, the reputation and sales of the magazine soared. It became the vanguard of the 1960s' satire boom, a movement that helped both create and reflect the irreverent spirit of the age.

The quintessence of Private Eye, *and of satire as a genre—castigating morals (in this case South African apartheid) by laughing at them.*

Aberfan

A small village some four miles south of Merthyr Tydfil in the coalmining district of South Wales, Aberfan was overhung by a vast mountain of pit waste, in the shadow of which stood Pantglas Junior School. At 9.15 a.m., after heavy overnight rain, a black avalanche suddenly poured down into the classrooms, and burst its way through a row of houses across the street. A total of 144 people died, swallowed up in soaking wet coal dust and rubble; 116 of them were local children.

In places, the landslip had piled up to nearly 40 feet. The back of the school was swept away, and only the gable ends of the adjoining wings stood above the black mire. Hundreds of distraught rescue workers, many of them professional miners, dug day and night, hoping against hope to find a survivor, but all they recovered were the bodies of those who had died, suffocated in a few brief seconds.

Strange tales began to emerge. Two weeks earlier, 10-year-old Eryl Mai Jones had told her mother Megan: "I am not afraid to die." When her mother gently told her that she was too young to think of death, Eryl replied: "But I shall be with my friends Peter and June." On the morning before the disaster, she told Megan of a dream. "I went to school, and there was no school there. Something black had come down all over it." When Eryl's body was eventually recovered, she was buried in a communal grave—between her friends Peter and June.

Psychiatrist Dr. J. C. Barker traveled to Aberfan, and there he heard Megan Jones's heartrending account. At his request, the London *Evening Standard* newspaper published an appeal for anyone who had experienced a similar forewarning of the disaster. Of the 76 replies that Dr. Barker himself received, he concluded that at least 60 were genuine, and in 24 cases the details had been related to others before the event. The most impressive account came from a woman living 300 miles from Aberfan, who had a detailed dream on October 14, and told a neighbor about it three days later. Dr. Barker announced his conviction that dreams could foreshadow coming events. But nothing had saved those tragic young lives. The Aberfan disaster resulted in an ambitious reclamation project, in which derelict land. All over Britain was transformed into landscaped parks and preserves.

Rescue workers search for bodies in the ruins of Pantglas school after a nearby heap of industrial waste slipped and buried it on October 21, 1966.

Florence Floods

The city of Florence is no stranger to devastating floods, as the surging waters of the Arno River rise above its retaining embankments. In the past, serious destruction had occurred in 1333 and 1557, but the most disastrous flood of modern times was that which took place on November 4, 1966. The water rapidly rose some 20 feet, and for several hours poured in a torrent through much of the historic center. Apart from the inevitable tons of mud and debris, a new—modern—threat came from oil that floated out of central-heating systems.

The destruction of public and private property was widespread, but the damage caused to irreplaceable works of art was even more serious. The collections in the Uffizi and Pitti galleries fortunately escaped any major defacement, but many churches and other museums (there are 40 in Florence) were devastated. The Etruscan collections in the Museo Archeologico, and Cimabue's *Crucifixion* in the Museo di Santa Croce were among the principal casualties. Two of Ghiberti's bronze doors on the Baptistry were badly damaged, and more than 1,000 panel paintings were submerged in the flood waters. The Vieusseux Library, with its 250,000 volumes, was obliterated, and several other libraries and archives were deep in mud and water.

If the techniques of art restoration had not reached their present-day level of skill, a significant proportion of the city's art treasures would have been lost for ever. An international rescue operation was mounted, and eventually a great number of the damaged works were repaired. Even Cimabue's *Crucifixion* hangs once more in its appointed place, guarded by an alarm system which, it is hoped, will go off in sufficient time for the painting to be moved in the event of a similar threat. The other works in Santa Croce have been removed to a higher floor.

Interviewed a few years ago, Professor Umberto Ballini, former head of the Department of Restoration in Florence, said: "I think that the Florentines will have to get used to living with floods, but people gradually tend to forget about such events... When Florence was flooded, it was a catastrophe because we were completely unprepared. We had forgotten."

An intrepid photographer takes a snapshot of the crumbling exterior of the Ponte Vecchio, the oldest bridge in Florence, as the waters of the Arno River rise to danger level in 1966.

First Super Bowl

On January 15, 1967, the Green Bay Packers became the first professional football champions by winning the inaugural Super Bowl between the winners of the newly formed American Football League (A.F.L.) and the long-established National Football League (N.F.L.).

One of the stars of the game was the Packers' Max McGee, who was renowned for his clowning and indiscipline. On the evening before the game, confident that he would not be required to play, he snuck out of the team camp, with a penalty of $5,000 hanging over his head if his absence was discovered. "I met some blonde the night before, and I was on my way to pay my respects," he later recalled. "I waddled in about 7.30 in the morning, and I could barely stand for the kick-off."

On the bench, McGee was asked by a team-mate what he would do if he had to play. "No way," McGee replied, "There's no way I could make it." At that moment, coach Vince Lombardi shouted "McGee! Get in the game!" "I played the rest of the game, and caught seven passes and scored two touchdowns.... I think Bart [Starr] intentionally threw the ball behind me.... When the ball stuck, I almost fainted. I expected to open my left hand and find a silver dollar."

As Lombardi hugged the ball at the end of the game, he said: "The Chiefs are a good team, but we wore 'em down.... And what can you say about a guy like McGee? This was one of his finest games." Packer quarterback Bart Starr—a future Football Hall-of-Famer—was voted most valuable player. Each of the Packers received $15,000 for the game; the Chiefs were paid only $7,500 a man.

Originally billed as a World Championship Game, this annual confrontation became known in 1969 as the Super Bowl. It is said that the name came about when the A.F.L.'s founder, Lamar Hunt, happened to see his daughter playing with her "Superball," a popular toy of the time made from silicone rubber that enabled it to bounce unusually high. Taken by the name, Hunt wondered: "Why not call our championship game the Super Bowl?" The title was good, but the viewing figures were even better. The Super Bowl jumped straight to the top of the sports television ratings, and has stayed there ever since.

Doug Hart (43), and Bob Skoronski (76) trail their coach, Vince Lombardi, off the field following the Green Bay Packers' 35–10 win over the Kansas City Chiefs.

Bluebird Crashes

January 4, 1967: The speed boat *Bluebird* flips over backward as it crosses Coniston Water, in the Lake District of England, at a speed of 300 m.p.h. during an attempt on the world water-speed record.

Donald Campbell, the pilot who was killed in the accident, was the son of Sir Arthur Campbell, the British racing driver who, during the 1930s, held world records on both land and water. In 1964 Donald matched his father's achievements when his car and his turbojet hydroplane—both named *Bluebird*, as had been his father's—broke existing land and water records in Australia. But, despite a near-fatal crash in an earlier *Bluebird* car in 1960, Donald Campbell was still unsatisfied. It is said that he was obsessed with his father's achievements, and determined to push himself ever further.

When Campbell announced that Coniston Water would be the site for his latest attempt to break his own record, many thought it an inauspicious choice. In 1951, he had struck a submerged obstacle in the lake, causing severe damage to *Bluebird*. On the other hand, he had subsequently broken his previous records several times on the same stretch of water, between 1955 and 1958. Perhaps he wanted to lay the ghost of the lake; perhaps he was obsessively trying to live up to his father.

As *Bluebird* sped across the lake, history repeated itself—once again the speed boat struck a submerged obstacle, probably a log. Campbell's last words, heard over the radio intercom as the hydroplane reared up, were "She's going, she's going." Then, in a huge shower of spray, *Bluebird* plunged into the depths.

In December 2000, divers testing underwater cameras found the wreckage of the hydroplane, half buried in a layer of silt at a depth of 150 feet. There was considerable argument as to whether it should be recovered, or left untouched because it was Campbell's last resting place, but at length permission was granted to salvage it. In March 2001, watched by Campbell's widow Toni, the shattered hull of *Bluebird* was raised to the surface. The rear of the hydroplane was intact, but the cockpit area was completely crushed. In August, D.N.A. analysis confirmed that the human remains in the wreckage were indeed those of the great British daredevil.

Donald Campbell had crashed his speedboat before on Coniston Water, but in January 1967 he tempted fate once too often, with tragic results.

The Boston Strangler

Albert DeSalvo was never tried for the Boston Strangler murders, but the killings stopped after his arrest on other charges in 1964. That, together with his 1967 jail confessions, led most people to the conclusion that he was the perpetrator. Yet others believed that DeSalvo was not—could not have been—the killer.

Between June 1962 and January 1964, 13 women living alone in and around Boston, Massachusetts, were sexually assaulted and strangled to death. The sadistic killer always left his trademark, a bow neatly tied around part of the victim's anatomy. In the fall of 1964, a woman reported a sexual assault in her apartment, and described her assailant. He was identified as 33-year-old Albert DeSalvo.

DeSalvo was already known to the police—but as a burglar and rapist, not as a murderer. He had been arrested for breaking and entering in 1958, and given a suspended sentence. He then began calling on attractive young women, claiming to work for a modeling agency and noting their vital statistics. He did not make overt advances, although he later claimed that many of the girls seduced him.

In March 1960, DeSalvo was arrested for a break-in, and admitted that he was the so-called "Measuring Man." He was sentenced to two years in prison, but released after 10 months. Henceforth he used a different modus operandi. Dressed in green overalls and posing as a maintenance man, he became more aggressive, tying up his victims and assaulting them. Police calculated that the "Green Man" committed hundreds of rapes; DeSalvo himself claimed there were more than a thousand.

In 1964, DeSalvo was sent to a mental institution. There another inmate became convinced that he was the Boston Strangler, and told his lawyer, F. Lee Bailey. Bailey then interviewed DeSalvo, who admitted being the wanted man. But there were no witnesses or corroborating forensic evidence, so DeSalvo was never charged.

In 1973, DeSalvo was stabbed to death in prison. Three inmates were charged with his murder, but twice the trials ended in hung juries. The suspicion remained that DeSalvo may have been a pathological confessor rather than a serial killer. In December 2001, forensic scientists announced that stains on the underwear of one of the victims did not match the D.N.A. of Albert DeSalvo.

Albert DeSalvo (center), already serving a life sentence for unrelated crimes, is escorted under police guard after confessing in jail to the infamous Boston Strangler murders.

Greek Colonels' Coup

The chain of events that led to a military coup began in March 1964, when Constantine II succeeded to the throne of Greece. In the following year, he dismissed the popular left-leaning prime minister, Georgios Papandreou. Weeks of unrest followed, particularly in the capital, Athens, and the unease was scarcely allayed by the eventual appointment of Stephen Stefanopoulos as a caretaker in Papandreou's place. Elections were due in May 1967, and it looked certain that Papandreou would be returned with a strong center-left coalition.

Two separate factions began plotting to frustrate Papandreou's probable return to power. One was a cabal of generals headed by the king. The other was a junta of colonels, who decided on a preemptive strike, and overthrew the caretaker government, setting up a military dictatorship in its place. The front man of the new regime was a civilian, Konstantinos Kollias, but the leader of the coup, and the power behind Kollias, was Colonel George Papadopoulos.

The new regime suspended Parliament, and restricted most civil liberties, banning—among other things—beards, miniskirts, and popular protest music. Some 45,000 alleged subversives were thrown into prison, and Papandreou himself died under house arrest in 1968. In December 1967, Constantine attempted a counter-coup, and when it failed he fled to Rome, Italy. (The Greek monarchy was abolished by decree in 1973.)

In the face of widespread condemnation of the actions of the military junta—although Washington privately approved its pro-American sentiments—some attempt was made to improve the public image of the regime. Colonel Papadopoulos was declared prime minister, and at length several political prisoners were granted amnesty. Many Greeks were at first hopeful that the corruption and inefficiency of previous governments was at an end, but the colonels' repressive rule continued, and popular unrest gradually increased. The military dictatorship survived for seven years, but was finally destabilized after it intervened to overthrow Archbishop Makarios in Cyprus, and Turkey invaded the Mediterranean island. Democracy and civilian rule in Greece were reestablished in July 1974.

Tanks rumble through the streets of Athens, Greece, on April 21, 1967, as the army seizes power to prevent the election of a leftist government.

Expo '67, Montreal

An American magazine described it as "The Big Blast Up North." In 1964, the Canadian province of Quebec had decided to hold a major international exhibition in Montreal to celebrate the centenary of Canada's confederation in 1867. On April 27, 1967, Expo '67 was officially opened by prime minister Lester Pearson. "We are witnesses today," he said, "to the fulfilment of one of the most daring acts of faith in Canadian enterprise and ability ever taken." The theme of the fair was "Man and his World," and some 90 countries and regions took part, many with their own lavish national pavilions.

The Montreal International and Universal Exposition (its full title) was built on two islands in the St. Lawrence River. One, the Ile Ste. Hélène, was natural, but enlarged to twice its size; the other, dubbed La Ronde, was specially constructed. A new bridge and subway were built to provide access, and three loops of monorail ran around the fair and even through the United States pavilion.

This pavilion was the most spectacular building in Expo '67. It was a giant geodesic dome, brainchild of the revolutionary American designer Buckminster Fuller, in partnership with Japanese architect Shoji Sodao. A threequarter sphere, it was 250 feet in diameter, and stood 137 feet high. Remarkably, its constructors did not work from drawn plans, merely tables of figures that defined the dimensions of the stainless steel alloy struts, which were color-coded to indicate how they should be riveted together. Thousands of triangular plexiglass panels were operated by 250 motors, opening and closing according to weather conditions. Although the complete structure weighed 600 tons, it was frequently lighter: as Fuller had predicted, warmed air inside gave the dome an intrinsic buoyancy.

The year 1967 was also the 50th anniversary of the Russian Revolution, and the Soviet pavilion, with sections devoted to space exploration and the development of nuclear energy—and with a 600-seat cinema—drew fascinated crowds. Although this pavilion and most of the others were removed at the end of the six-month fair, several others were retained on site, and an annual "Man and his World" exhibition was held each summer until 1981.

The U.S.-Japanese geodesic dome that formed the centerpiece of Expo '67. The success of the fair was at least partly attributable to the high level of international cooperation.

The Six-Day War

Serious conflict between Arabs and Israelis began in 1948, when the state of Israel was declared, and forces from Egypt, Jordan, Iraq, Syria, and Lebanon entered Palestine "to restore order." Sporadic confrontation has continued ever since.

Refugee Palestinians formed guerrilla groups, regularly attacking Israeli settlements. In 1964, Egyptian president Gamal Abdal Nasser attempted to control these independent forces by combining them in the Palestinian Liberation Organization (P.L.O.), but their attacks, supported by Syria, grew ever more violent. In May 1967, Israel began to mass troops on the Syrian frontier, and Nasser reacted forcefully. He ordered U.N. peacekeeping troops to leave the Egyptian border with Israel, blockaded the Red Sea, and made a military pact with Jordan. Syria, Jordan, Iraq, Kuwait—and distant Algeria—then announced that they would "wipe Israel off the map" if it retaliated.

The Israelis, anticipating an imminent invasion, reacted swiftly. On June 5, they established air supremacy, virtually destroying the Egyptian air force and its airfields. Similar damage was done to Syrian and Jordanian air power. On the following day, Israeli armor took the Gaza Strip and advanced deep into the Sinai Peninsula, while ground troops surrounded the Old City of Jerusalem and entered the West Bank territory of Jordan.

On June 7, Egyptian resistance collapsed in Sinai, and Israeli forces advanced unopposed to the Gulf of Suez. The whole city of Jerusalem fell to the army, and in the north Nablus and Jericho were captured. Israel and Jordan acceded to a U.N. call for a ceasefire, and next day a ceasefire between Egypt and Israel came into force. Then the Israelis attacked Syrian artillery positions, and advanced 12 miles into Syrian territory, before a further ceasefire was agreed. In just six days, Israel had defeated the forces of its three neighbors, and had not only occupied a considerable area of land, but had also established the reputation of the army and air force as formidable fighters. "Plucky little Israel" was the phrase on many Western lips. In November 1967, the U.N. Security Council unanimously passed a British resolution calling for Israeli withdrawal from the territories they had occupied, but to no avail.

An Israeli tank advances against Syria over the Golan Heights toward the end of the Six-Day War of June 5–10, 1967.

The Summer of Love

In the spring of 1967, protest against the war in Vietnam was increasing, not only in the United States but across the world. People of all classes—rock stars, leading writers, suburban home-owners, radical academics—came together to promulgate a New Age, with its slogan "make love, not war." On April 15, 300,000 demonstrators marched in New York to inaugurate the "Summer of Love." Among them were Dr. Benjamin Spock, the pediatrician; folk singer Pete Seeger; and Martin Luther King, Jr., who, addressing the vast crowd, stressed the connection between the struggle for peace and the struggle for racial equality.

"Flower power" became the slogan of the summer. "All You Need Is Love" sang The Beatles, surrounded by flowers and floating balloons, in a worldwide television broadcast, less than two weeks after the Arab-Israeli Six-Day War.

Thousands of hippie "flower children" were converging on the Haight-Ashbury district of San Francisco—known, significantly, to its new residents as "Hashbury." They organized a succession of "be-ins," "love-ins," and "smoke-ins." Wrote Professor Lewis Yablonsky: "It is almost a fantasy land of sights and sounds. Flute-players in robes. Micro-minied girls in boots, without bras... swing down the streets.'"

The movement reached its high point with the First Annual International Pop Festival, which opened at Monterey, California on June 16. The "annual" label never materialized, and the"'international" part did not mean the inclusion of either The Beatles or The Rolling Stones—Mick Jagger and Keith Richards had just been charged with drug offenses, and Brian Jones attended only as a guest. But The Who came from Britain, with Jimi Hendrix, and Eric Burdon and the Animals. Canada contributed an obscure group, The Paupers; Ravi Shankar, from India, and Hugh Masakela, from South Africa, also appeared.

For three days, the sound of tinkling bells about the necks of the audience was drowned by the storming music from the stage. The cloud from innumerable joints was matched by Pete Townshend's smoke bombs; and then Hendrix went one better, setting fire to his guitar. But then it was all over, and flower power declined into drug abuse and petty crime.

Californian hippies take pop singer Scott McKenzie's advice: "If you're going to San Francisco, Be sure to wear some flowers in your hair."

QE2

September 20, 1967: Queen Elizabeth II of England gave her name to the new £30-million Cunard liner on the day of its launch at the John Brown Shipyard in Glasgow, Scotland.

By the mid 1950s, the great shipping companies were facing severe competition from airlines, especially on the transatlantic routes between Europe and North America. Passengers had the choice of making the crossing in less than eight hours in a plane, or in four to five days by ship. And over longer distances—to South America or Australia, for example—the contrast was even greater. Soon, the great passenger ships were losing money, and were gradually withdrawn from service: the *Queen Mary* in 1967, the *Queen Elizabeth* and the *United States* in 1969.

However, there remained a hard core of travelers who preferred the comfort and relaxation of a ship, while there was a growing business in holiday cruises. Shipowners hit on the idea of dual-purpose vessels that could continue the transatlantic trade during the summer months and provide luxury cruising accommodation in the winter. One of the most famous of these was the Cunard Line's *Queen Elizabeth 2*, known universally as the QE2.

The QE2 was smaller than its famous predecessors—although, weighing 65,000 tons and measuring 963 feet from stem to stern, it was still a big ship, capable of carrying 1,700 passengers. Most importantly, however, it was given a draft of less than 32 feet, so that it would be able to enter some of the world's shallowest harbors. The design of the hull made use of the latest techniques, and all the upperworks were constructed of light alloy. Passenger facilities included five restaurants and two cafés, four swimming pools, and a 480-seater cinema.

The QE2 made its maiden voyage from Southampton, England, to New York in May 1969. The *Queen Mary*, now obsolete, was sold to the city of Long Beach, California, in 1967, where it was moored offshore as the Hotel Queen Mary. The *Queen Elizabeth*, now also superfluous to its owners' requirements, was taken to Hong Kong. The plan was to convert it into a floating university, but the liner was destroyed by fire in 1972.

The QE2 dwarves the surrounding buildings as Queen Elizabeth II, after whom the ship is named, prepares to break the ceremonial bottle of champagne across the bow.

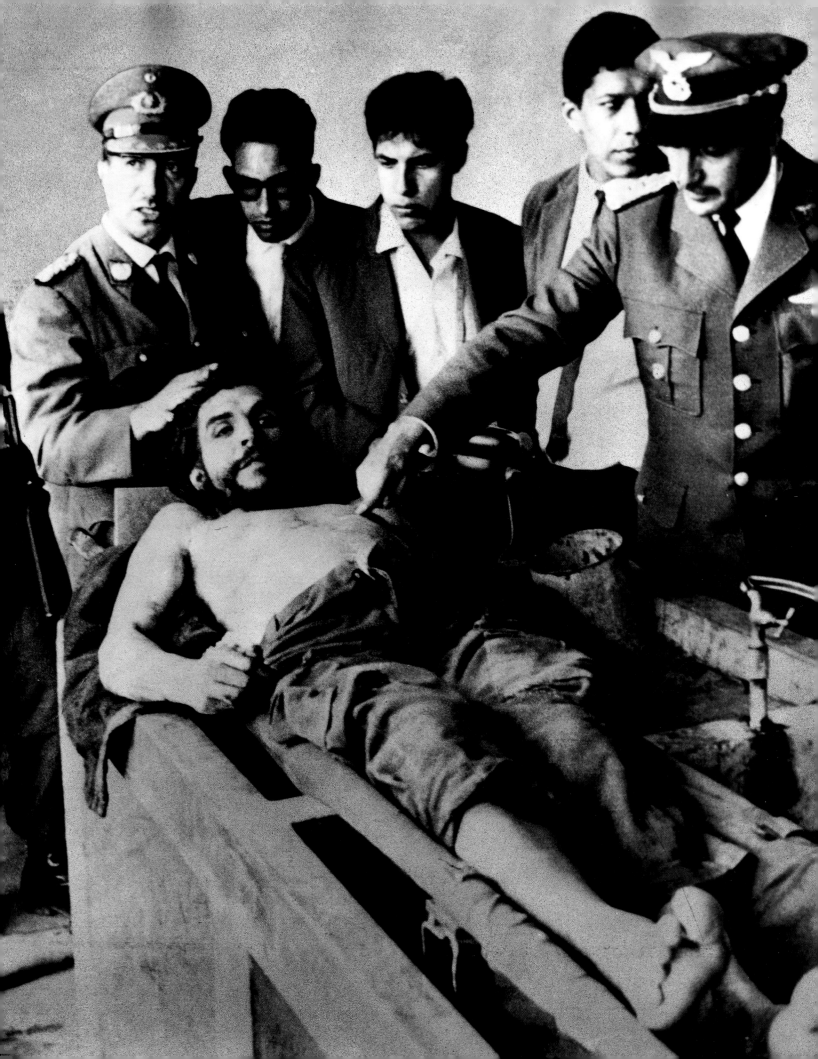

The Death of Che

Che Guevara (1928–1967) was a violent revolutionary who devoted his life to the liberation of Latin American nations from the forces of imperialism.

Born into a prosperous middle-class family in Argentina, and trained as a doctor, Che Guevara was an unlikely revolutionary. He had traveled for some time in South America before he met the young lawyer Fidel Castro in Mexico in 1955. Castro had been exiled from his native Cuba for his part in a failed coup to overthrow the brutal dictator Juan Battista, and was now planning a second attempt. With Guevara as his trusted lieutenant, he returned in 1956 and, after a bitter guerrilla campaign, drove out Battista on the first day of 1959.

Following the success of the Cuban revolution, Che Guevara wrote a handbook, *Guerrilla Warfare* (1961), which has been favorably compared to that by No Nguyen Giap, the Vietnamese freedom fighter. Che was later appointed director of the Cuban National Bank, where he imposed a ruthless Soviet-style economy.

At this time press photographer Alberto Diaz Gutierrez (known as "Korda") was in Havana to cover the ceremonial interment of victims of *La Coubre*, a French cargo vessel that had mysteriously exploded while carrying arms to Cuba. With his telephoto lens, Korda shot pictures of Castro and those with him on the platform; for a few seconds, Guevara, in his revolutionary's beret, emerged from the back to view the huge crowd, and Korda was able to secure just two photographs.

In 1965, Guevara suddenly disappeared from Cuba, provoking an intensive manhunt by Western intelligence agencies. He was rumored to be in Panama, training guerrilla groups; plotting a rising in Peru; leading rebels in Colombia; on a political mission to Vietnam. He was, in fact, leading the fight against white mercenaries in the Congo. Finally, in 1967, he reemerged in Bolivia in command of a guerrilla battalion. In October the Bolivian army, assisted by the C.I.A., caught up with him, and a few days later he was shot.

One of the two photos taken by Korda in 1960, and which he had almost forgotten, was immediately printed as a poster by an Italian publisher, and the image of Che became an icon that is still to be seen around the world.

The body of Ernesto Guevara de la Serna—known to the world as the guerrilla leader Che—lies in a Bolivian morgue four days after his execution on October 9, 1967.

Warhol and Monroe

By the end of 1967, pop artist Andy Warhol was at the height of his fame, and a major retrospective in Manhattan, New York, was to be the crowning moment of a high-profile career.

Warhol was born in Pittsburgh, Pennsylvania, in 1928, the third son of immigrants from Ruthenia (now part of Slovakia). After art training, he moved to New York in 1949, where he worked as a commercial illustrator for 13 years. In 1960, he started to produce paintings based on comic-strip images; but, discovering that Roy Lichtenstein was doing the same sort of work, he turned to a series of 32 paintings of Campbell's Soup cans.

Warhol's cans immediately earned him membership of the "Pop art" movement. In 1962, the year he finally gave up commercial art, he used the advertising technique of silk-screen printing to produce his "Marilyn Diptych"—50 modified photographs, in color and black-and-white, of the actress Marilyn Monroe, who had just died. He followed this with similar portraits of Elvis Presley.

Advised to pursue darker subjects, Warhol then embarked on his "Disaster" series: fatal car crashes, race riots, and—notoriously—the electric chair. He set up his New York studio in 1963 in a loft on East 47th Street, where his screen-printing machinery and numerous working assistants soon earned it the name of The Factory. He bought a 16-millimeter camera and began making "underground" movies, such as *Sleep*, *Eat*, and *Blow Job*. Soon he was a famous gay icon, his head topped with a wild blonde wig, and he attracted a glamorous following of people who gave themselves names such as "Ingrid Superstar," and "Ultra Violet."

In 1965 Warhol announced that he would be devoting more of his energies to film-making. He also promoted the rock band The Grateful Dead, and designed the sleeve for The Rolling Stones' album *Sticky Fingers*.

At the time of this snapshot, Warhol was the toast of the town, but on June 3 the following year he was shot in the street by Valerie Solanas, a wannabe actress. He was hospitalized for eight weeks, and never recovered fully from his injuries. His star faded. Andy Warhol died in February 1987, following a gall bladder operation.

December 1967: American pop artist Andy Warhol hangs his transparent Marilyn Monroe at the exhibition in New York City.

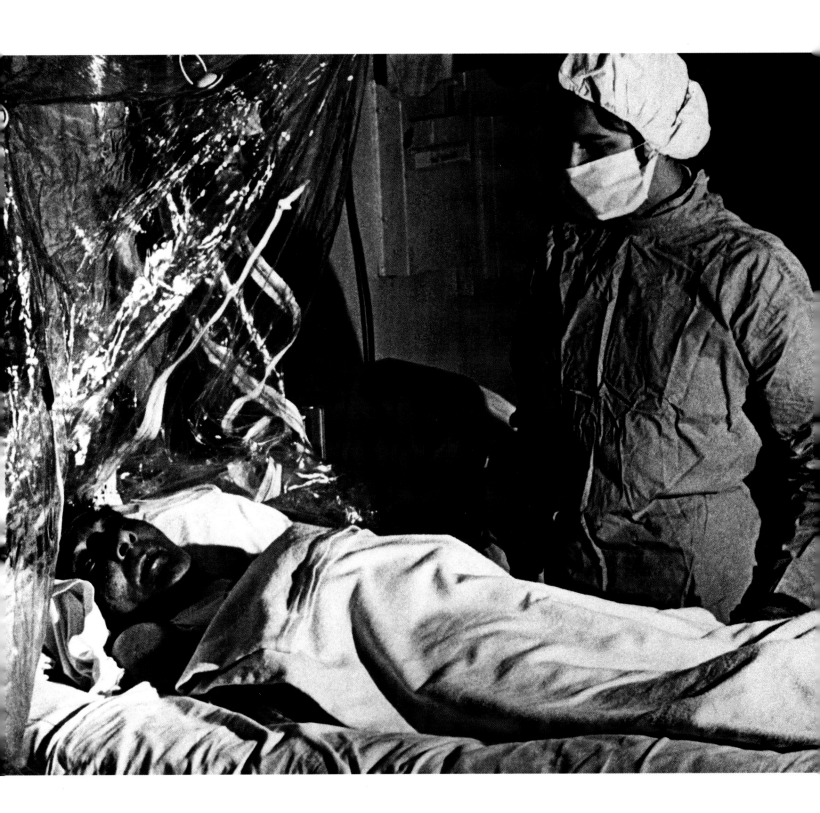

The First Heart Transplant

On December 3, 1967, the first successful heart transplant was performed on 55-year-old Louis Washkansky by a team of 30 doctors at the Groote Schuur Hospital in Cape Town, South Africa, under the direction of South African surgeon Christiaan Barnard.

Transplantation of human tissues—skin, bone, or cartilage—had become well-established during the first half of the 20th century, and even the replacement of a limb proved successful in a few cases, but transplantation of organs such as the heart seemed almost unimaginable. However, this was the historic day on which the impossible proved possible.

The organ donor was Denise Darvall, a 25-year-old woman who had been fatally injured in a car crash—her head and body were severely damaged, but her heart was untouched and still beating. Barnard obtained permission to attempt his revolutionary experimental surgery, then cut through Washkansky's breastbone and eased his ribs aside, incising the pericardial sac to reveal the gray, swollen organ within, while a heart-lung machine kept the blood flowing through the patient's body, bypassing his heart.

About 95 percent of the heart was cut away, leaving the top of the organ in place. Then a matching part of Denise Darvall's healthy heart was sewn onto this upper portion. Twin electrodes were attached to the transplanted organ, and an electric shock given to start it beating again: "It was like turning on the ignition of a car," said a member of the team later, as Washkansky's new heart began to pump blood once more around his body. Only hours later, the patient and Barnard met in the recovery room. "You promised me a new heart," said Washansky in a faint whisper. Barnard smiled: "You've got a new heart," he replied.

Unfortunately, Washkansky developed pneumonia, and died 18 days later; but the new technique blazed a trail. Before Barnard's breakthrough, many people believed that vital organs were irreplaceable, but today heart transplants are commonplace, and patients have a life expectancy of many years. In 1974, Barnard became the first surgeon to implant a second heart in a human being, and to link the hearts to work together to provide blood circulation.

Fifty-five-year-old Louis Washkansky recuperates after receiving the world's first successful heart transplant in December 1967.

Burn the Draft

American involvement in Vietnam escalated after March 1965, when President Johnson authorized the bombing of the North, and began to send in ground forces, as distinct from "military advisers." By the end of the year, there were 180,000 U.S. combat troops in Vietnam, and many young Americans faced the possibility of being drafted to serve in a war of which they did not approve.

Yet opposition to the Vietnam War had been initiated, not by students, but by a group of academics at the University of Michigan, Ann Arbor. They became incensed when the State Department "had the gall to treat them like children," answering their letters with pamphlets explaining the diabolical nature of communism, and illustrated by a leering Khrushchev. Their response was to hold a "teach-in" at the university, which was attended by a crowd of more than 3,000 people during the night of March 24–25.

In the following three months, more than 100 similar events were held on campuses all over the United States. At Berkeley, California, in the largest of the teach-ins, the son of a professor made the symbolic gesture of tearing up his draft card. As a result, a law was swiftly passed making the destruction of draft cards a Federal offense. Former president Eisenhower deplored the "moral deterioration" of American youth; the president of Yale University described the "tragedy" of "college rebels "who "hurt their own cause when they demonstrate first, and think about it later."

The director of the Selective Service System, General Lewis Hershey, then deliberately revoked the deferment of 30 students. Young men who failed their grades, or dropped out of university, found themselves faced with conscription. In a New York demonstration, a Roman Catholic pacifist named David Miller publicly burned his draft card, for which he was imprisoned for two years—but his gesture was soon repeated all over the United States by numerous others, including the protester shown here. He was one of 100,000 people who marched through Washington, D.C., on October 21, 1967. During this demonstration, young women placed flowers in the gun barrels of soldiers guarding government buildings, and hundreds of young men stood in line and urinated in the direction of the Pentagon.

A demonstrator sets fire to his military draft card during an anti-Vietnam War protest march through the U.S. capital in October 1967.

The *Pueblo* Incident

The Korean War, in which the United Nations, led by the United States, had attempted to drive communist invaders out of South Korea, ended in an inconclusive ceasefire in 1953, but the United States continued to maintain a security force of 55,000 men in South Korea.

Thereafter, North Korea kept up a lively propaganda war against its southern neighbor, and also increasingly allowed guerrilla groups to slip across the border and raid cities in South Korea. By the mid-1960s, these incursions were seen by Washington as part of a communist plot to undermine the war in Vietnam, in which the United States was already facing defeat. In an effort to monitor and anticipate North Korean actions, the U.S. Navy stationed spy ships, packed with electronic equipment, in international waters off the Korean coast.

One of these was the *Pueblo*, which the North Koreans impounded in January, claiming that the ship had entered their territorial waters in the Sea of Japan and was "carrying out hostile activities." Washington protested that the action was "a wanton and aggressive act."

U.S. president Lyndon Johnson decided that negotiations were preferable to military intervention, but they became long and drawn-out, and the American sailors eventually remained in prison for nearly a year. They were frequently beaten, and many "confessed" that the *Pueblo* had indeed been within North Korean territorial waters. Even the ship's captain, Commander Lloyd M. Bucher, signed a confession—in order, he later said, to protect the lives of his men.

Eventually, the United States apologized to North Korea, but in an extraordinarily equivocal way. In a procedure unprecedented in international law, the Americans denounced the document in which they admitted spying as false before they signed it. The principal American negotiator later stressed that this was "to free the crew, and only to free the crew."

The sailors were given a heroes' welcome on their return to the United States, and the incident was quietly dismissed as an unfortunate embarrassment. But the North Koreans kept the *Pueblo*.

On February 5, 1968, high school students in Seoul, South Korea, protest the capture on January 23 by North Korea of the U.S. ship Pueblo, and the imprisonment of its crew of 83.

The Tet Offensive

The North Vietnamese onslaught on South Vietnam during a religious holiday at the start of 1968 was a short-term failure, but it taught the Americans that this was a war they could not win.

After three years of all-out war, the Pentagon declared confidently that most of South Vietnam was "secured," and that there was "light at the end of the tunnel." Then, taking advantage of the holiday disruption of Tet, the Buddhist New Year, more than 60,000 North Vietnamese attacked across the whole country. Hoping (vainly, as it turned out) to spark a popular uprising in their favor, they even struck at the heart of Saigon, and captured the old citadel in Hue.

General Fred Weygand, U.S. commander in the Saigon area, had several battalions in reserve nearby and, after fierce urban fighting, the city was cleared within a week, as were most of the other towns. Hue, however, took a month to subdue. The U.S. Air Force bombed the ancient city to ruins, while the town of Ben Tre, south of Saigon, was completely destroyed by American troops—as one army officer famously declared, "to save it."

Although the offensive was acknowledged a military failure—the Viet Cong and North Vietnamese Army suffered nearly 30,000 casualties during the fighting—it was nevertheless a psychological disaster for the United States. Abroad, the credibility of the American administration, and its policy of steady attrition of the North Vietnamese forces, was ruined. The Viet Cong—who, dressed as civilians, had been smuggling arms into Saigon in coffins and flowerpots—could clearly count on thousands of sympathizers in South Vietnam.

At once there was a dramatic reversal in U.S. policy. When General William Westmoreland, the American commander, requested a further 206,000 troops, President Johnson authorized only 13,500, and shortly afterward relieved Westmoreland of his command. Johnson then declared a partial halt to the bombing of North Vietnam, thus persuading the Viet Cong to attend peace talks—or, at least, "talks about talks"—in Paris, France. The U.S. president then announced that he would not be seeking reelection—Tet had brought about his political downfall.

January 30, 1968: Black smoke billows over central Saigon as the Viet Cong launch a huge, concerted attack on South Vietnam.

My Lai

The aftermath of the Tet offensive in South Vietnam resulted in one of the worst scandals ever to darken the reputation of the U.S. Army. On March 16, 1968, Charlie Company of the 11th Brigade approached the small village of My Lai. The village was in the bitterly contested region of Quang Ngai on the northeast coast of South Vietnam, where during the previous weeks many members of Charlie Company had been wounded or killed by Viet Cong landmines. "This is what you've been waiting for," announced one of the officers gleefully, "search and destroy—and you've got it."

Lieutenant William Calley ordered his men to enter My Lai firing, even though there was no sign of opposing fire and there were no Viet Cong hiding there. The soldiers, angry and frustrated, quickly made up for their disappointment by massacring more than 300 unarmed civilians, including women, children, and old men. Some were bayoneted, praying women and children were shot in the back of the head, and at least one girl was raped before being killed. Calley himself rounded up a group of villagers, ordered them into a ditch, and despatched them with a furious burst of automatic gunfire. Military photographers then made a record of the soldiers' handiwork.

The American public did not learn of the massacre until November 1969, when a journalist published details of his conversations with Vietnam veteran Ron Ridenhour. But Calley, as a result of Ridenhour's appeals to Congress and the Pentagon, had already been charged with murder by the Army two months earlier. A commission of enquiry concluded that, as professional soldiers in Vietnam were gradually withdrawn from combat or retired, the Army had come to rely more and more on draftees with little or no military experience, and poor leadership skills.

Calley was an unemployed college dropout, who had graduated from officer training school in 1967. At his trial, he claimed that he had been ordered by his superior officer to kill everyone in My Lai, but the court found insufficient evidence to convict anyone else. Calley was sentenced to life imprisonment, but released in 1974, and given a dishonorable discharge from the Army.

The My Lai massacre, photographed by U.S. cameramen. This was not an isolated incident: at about the same time, the U.S. Army wiped out all the civilians in the village of My Khe.

Paris Student Riots

A time of protest, 1968 became known as "the year of the barricades." Students and workers rose up against the establishment in Spain, Poland, Mexico, Japan, Italy, West Germany, Belgium, Yugoslavia, Britain, and the United States. Red Guards battled in Beijing, China, and Warsaw Pact forces invaded Czechoslovakia. But the event that caught the popular imagination of the Western world more than any other took place in France in May.

The trouble began at the university of Nanterre, to the east of Paris. Daniel Cohn-Bendit was a sociology student there; born in 1945, he had taken German citizenship in 1959 to avoid French military service. There was much unrest among the students because they wanted greater control of the university. On March 22, Cohn-Bendit led a band of protesters into the university conference chamber; the university was closed for three days, and he and seven others were summoned to appear at a disciplinary hearing in the Sorbonne on May 6.

When the Nanterre students arrived in Paris, a group of some 500 students demonstrated in their support on May 3. The rector of the Sorbonne called for police assistance, and many of the demonstrators were arrested. That sparked off an immediate reaction. Militant students, joined by many more with no previous record of violence, began to dig up the cobblestones: some of these they used to build barricades, the rest were hurled at the police, who responded with batons and teargas grenades. The violence of the following days provoked outrage throughout France. Students in other universities rose up in protest, a general strike was declared, and seven million workers occupied their factories. Many feared the start of a second French Revolution.

After 10 days of increasingly violent confrontation in Paris, the rector announced the reopening of the Sorbonne. But the result was not what he expected: the students immediately occupied the university buildings. Paris ground to a standstill, and remained in near-paralysis for six weeks. French broadcasting stations were closed down, and petrol rationing was introduced. Industrial unrest continued into July. The whole episode became known simply as *les événements* ("the events').

Street fighting between students and security police on the Boulevard St. Michel in Paris, France, two days after the end of the student occupation of the Sorbonne in June 1968.

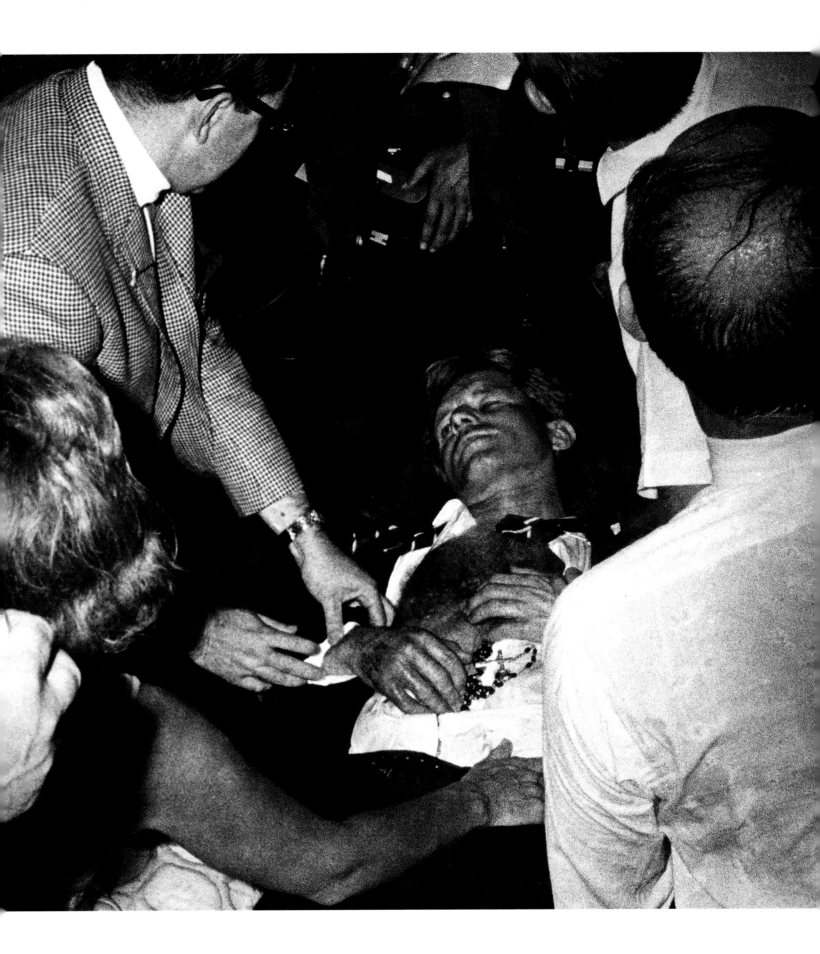

R.F.K. Assassinated

When John Kennedy was assassinated in 1963, his mantle fell on the shoulders of his younger brother Robert. "Bobby" had gained a reputation as a fearsome crime-fighter while chief counsel for the Senate Rackets Committee (1957–1960). His appointment as attorney general in the Kennedy administration in 1961, at the age of 36, was seen by some as blatant nepotism, but his work on the Civil Rights Act in 1964 secured his standing as a legislator. The road to the White House looked open.

Bobby was elected Democrat U.S. senator for New York State in 1964, and became a fierce opponent of the bombing of North Vietnam. On November 30, 1967, Democrat senator Eugene McCarthy decided to run as a presidential candidate in the forthcoming election. In the first primary, in March 1968, McCarthy nearly defeated President Johnson, and it was then that Kennedy announced his own candidacy. When, a few days later, the news came that Johnson would not be seeking reelection, the primaries became a ding-dong battle between McCarthy and Kennedy. As the results of the California primary began to come in at around 11 p.m. on June 4, it became clear that Kennedy was pulling ahead.

That evening, Bobby had—rather reluctantly—come to the Democrats' election night party at the Ambassador Hotel. From his suite he took a service elevator to the kitchen, walked through the pantry, and was greeted by ecstatic applause. After a rousing speech, he set off back for a news conference. As he pushed through the packed crowd in the pantry, a small man pulled out a revolver and fired blindly in his direction. Four of Kennedy's aides were wounded, and he fell, dying, to the floor.

The small man was Sirhan Bishara Sirhan, an apprentice jockey of Arab origin. There is no question that he was drunk, and his motive for the assassination has been debated for years. It has been said that he killed Kennedy because of the senator's support for Israel, but Sirhan was a Christian, and he himself claimed that he could remember almost nothing of the evening's events.

Sirhan Sirhan was put on trial for the murder of Bobby Kennedy, and sentenced to death; later, with the abolition of capital punishment in California, this was commuted to life imprisonment.

Clutching his rosary beads, Senator Robert F. Kennedy lies dying on the floor of the Ambassador Hotel, Los Angeles, California, on June 8, 1968.

Rape of Czechoslovakia

Between 1948 and 1989, Czechoslovakia (now two separate countries, the Czech Republic and Slovakia) was a Soviet satellite state. Many Czechs hated life under communism, and there were increasingly public displays of discontent with censorship and the economy. In October 1967, Alexander Dubcek, first secretary of the Slovak Communist Party, mounted a fierce attack on the state of the nation, and in January 1968 he was elected first secretary of the national party. Antonin Novotny remained president, however, and planned a military coup to regain his authority. When the plan failed, he resigned on March 22. General Ludvik Svoboda was elected in his place, and a new government was formed on April 8.

Two days later, the new leadership announced an "action program," declaring that Czechoslovakia would remain a socialist state but promising "socialism with a human face." Censorship was abolished, and political prisoners were released. It was the beginning of the "Prague spring."

It did not last long, however. Dubcek and deputy premier Oldrich Cernik were summoned to Moscow, and ordered to toe the line. Then the Soviets decided that only force would resolve the situation. On August 20, 1968, they sent in a joint force of Soviet, Polish, East German, Hungarian, and Bulgarian military units. Dubcek, Cernik, and Josef Smrkovsky, chairman of the National Assembly, were arrested, denounced as traitors, and carried off to Moscow—Dubcek in handcuffs.

The invaders were amazed by the hostility with which they were received. In Bratislava, a Russian soldier spoke to the protesting crowd. The soldiers, he said, were intelligent and sympathized with the people—but their officers and politicians were stupid, and the soldiers could do nothing.

President Svoboda flew to Moscow, but refused to negotiate until his colleagues were released. He returned with them to Prague a week later, but this was no more than a gesture of defiance; in reality his nation was already defeated. On October 16 an agreement was signed allowing 70,000 Soviet troops to remain on Czech soil. Although the Czechs and Slovaks resisted the occupation with the limited means at their disposal, it was 20 years before the nation finally threw off the Soviet yoke.

Just over a week after the Soviet Union invaded Czechoslovakia in August 1968, youths in the capital, Prague, climb on a wrecked Russian tank.

French Pacific H-Bomb

September 8, 1968: In the face of a storm of international protests, France exploded an H-bomb in a remote part of the South Pacific Ocean. This was the second such test the French had carried out in a month.

When the Limited Test Ban Treaty was agreed in 1964, two major nations refused to sign: France and China. The reason for this soon became clear: while Britain, the United States, and the Soviet Union had all successfully developed a thermonuclear "hydrogen" bomb, France and China were lagging behind. China was not yet a nuclear power, and although France had held many successful atomic bomb tests in Algeria, and would carry out more in the Pacific, development of a French H-bomb appeared to be at a standstill.

That all changed in October 1964, when China became the fifth nation to explode an atomic bomb. French president de Gaulle suddenly jolted his scientists into action. "It's of capital importance," he declared. "Of the five nuclear powers, are we going to be the only one that hasn't made it to the thermonuclear level? Are we going to let the Chinese get ahead of us?... 1968 at the latest—figure it out!"

Frantic theoretical work ensued, but it was not until 1967 that Sir William Cook, former director of the Atomic Research Establishment at Aldermaston, England, arrived in Paris, France, and provided information that validated one of the French theoretical models. Two devices were then planned within days, one with a yield of several megatons (a megaton being the explosive force of a million tons of T.N.T.), and a smaller one of a single megaton. By August 1968, both were ready for testing.

The two bombs were transported to Papeete, one of a group of small islands (formerly French Polynesia) in the centre of the South Pacific, and were exploded from balloons, the idea being that the radioactive fallout would be dispersed over a wide area of open sea. The first test, on August 24, was successful, but nothing could be seen of it because the explosion was obscured by thick cloud. However, the second took place in perfectly clear weather, and provided photographs that were published by the media around the world. France had regained her position among the nuclear powers.

The second French H-bomb provided spectacular photographs, but Polynesian islanders wondered why the Europeans did not carry out their tests closer to home.

Black Power Olympics

October 27, 1968: The winners of the 200-meters final at the Mexico City Olympics stood on the rostrum before the American flag, as "The Star Spangled Banner" was played. Gold medallist Tommie Smith and bronze medallist John Carlos had approached the podium shoeless in black socks. When the award ceremony began, they bowed their heads, and each raised a black-gloved fist high in the Black Power salute. In his left hand, Smith carried a box containing an olive branch, to symbolize peace; while in Carlos's right hand was a knotted black silk scarf, representing lynching.

Two years earlier, Stokely Carmichael had addressed a crowd of 3,000 in a park in Mississippi with a fiery speech in which he made famous the term "Black Power." The following year he joined the Black Panthers, an armed urban movement founded by Huey Newton and Bobby Seale. Its members wore black berets, and raised their fists in a salute reminiscent both of the Bolsheviks and of the Anarchists. As Smith said later: "It was the fist that scared people. White folks would have forgiven the black socks, the silk scarf, the bowed head. But they saw that raised black fist and were afraid."

This gesture by Tommie Smith and John Carlos, which they had innocently planned as a nonviolent demonstration, provoked international outrage. One of the few public figures who was not scandalized was the boxer Muhammad Ali, who described it as "the single most courageous act of this century." The two sprinters were immediately expelled from the Olympic village; thereafter, they received death threats, and had sponsorship offers withdrawn. The pressure took a heavy toll on their loved ones: Smith's wife sued for divorce, while Carlos's wife committed suicide. One of the greatest athletes of the time, with 11 world records to his credit, Smith was banned from track events, and reduced to playing minor league football for three seasons.

At last, Santa Monica College, California, hired Tommie Smith as a trainer: "Now, future athletes come into my office and see the photo. 'Is that you, sir?' they ask. And I explain how that gesture destroyed my life, but helped build my country."

Smith and Carlos showing their support for the civil rights' campaign. Their gesture was taken as an incitement to violence. (The silver medallist is Peter Norman of Australia.)

Nixon Elected

Although Republican Richard M. Nixon had been defeated by John Kennedy in the 1960 presidential election, he came back to win at the second attempt. Although his term of office was eventful, nothing was as momentous as the manner in which he eventually left the White House.

From 1952, when he was aged only 39, until 1960, Nixon had served as Vice-President to Dwight D. Eisenhower. Acknowledged a brilliant lawyer, he had already achieved notoriety as a member of Senator Joseph McCarthy's Un-American Activities Committee, which destroyed the careers of many well-known Americans.

Nixon's 1968 campaign was helped partly by the turmoil into which the Democrats had been thrown after the assassination of Robert Kennedy, who had generally been regarded as the frontrunner for the party's nomination. When President Johnson announced that he would not seek reelection, Vice-President Hubert Humphrey announced his own candidacy, and was nominated at a wildly enthusiastic convention in Chicago, Illinois.

The other contender in a three-cornered fight was the anti-integrationist George Wallace, governor of Alabama. The American Independent Party, for which Wallace stood, also benefited Nixon because it took votes from the Democrats in the South.

The 1968 election was a hard-fought campaign. For some time Nixon led the field but, as Humphrey became steadily more critical of Johnson's handling of the Vietnam War, the lead began to narrow. However, it did not reduce sufficiently to prevent a Republican victory.

During his first administration, Nixon gained widespread approval by abolishing the draft and engineering American withdrawal from Vietnam. In 1972, having announced that he was seeking a second term, he visited Beijing and Moscow, and thus reduced tension between China, the Soviet Union, and the United States.

Soon after his reelection, the "Watergate" scandal broke, following a break-in at the Democrats' offices in Washington, D. C. Although Nixon denied involvement, he was forced to surrender tape recordings that implicated him in the burglary. Threatened with impeachment, he resigned on August 9, 1974.

Richard Nixon on the campaign trail. Despite winning all but four states west of the Mississippi, his overall victory margin was only about 500,000 votes, or one percent.

Jan Palach

At 2.30 p.m. on January 16, 1969, Jan Palach, a 20-year-old philosophy student at Charles University in Prague, Czechoslovakia, deliberately set fire to himself in the city's Wenceslas Square in protest at the Soviet invasion of his country, and what he saw as the weak-kneed attitude of the Czech government.

As he lay in hospital, dying of his dreadful burns, Palach begged the people gathered round his bed to make sure the world knew that his death was not a suicide, but a determined demonstration against the plight of Czechoslovakia.

In 1963, a Buddhist monk had immolated himself in a similar way in central Saigon, in protest against the dictatorship of South Vietnamese president Diem, and Palach maintained that his act was in the Buddhist tradition. He had turned himself into a human torch, both literally and metaphorically—the torch of freedom.

On the day that Palach was buried, an estimated crowd of 800,000 turned out onto the streets of Prague. His grave was visited daily by people with flowers until the authorities removed his body to a secret plot outside the capital.

While Jan Palach is still remembered to this day, two other brave Czechs who followed his example are almost forgotten. The first was another student, 18-year-old Jan Zajic, who began a hunger strike in Wenceslas Square in support of Palach's protest. When he was ignored by the authorities, he turned himself—as he put it in his farewell letter—into "Torch Number Two." On February 25, he burned to death in the square.

On April 4, 40-year-old technician Evzen Plocek met the same terrible death in the main square of the town of Jihlava. Between January and April 1969, no fewer than 26 Czechs set themselves on fire, and seven of them died. Prague sources confess that they are unclear how many had aims "as noble as those of Palach, Zajic, and Plocek," and how many were suffering from personal problems. "But," they say, "the memory of those who decided to put their death in the service of truth guided many Czechs through the hopeless decades of the Communist dictatorship. Their selfless act shaped the Czech conscience during the 20-year period between 1969 and 1989, and changed it forever."

A mourner at the funeral of Jan Palach. Every year on the anniversary of his death, a solemn wreath-laying ceremony takes place on the spot where he set fire to himself.

John and Yoko Bed In

March 27, 1969: Beatle John Lennon, and his wife of a week, Yoko Ono, receive the press at their bedside in the presidential suite of the Hilton Hotel, Amsterdam, Netherlands. The couple stayed in bed for seven days "as a protest against war and violence in the world."

Who is Yoko Ono? Beatles' fans began to ask in 1967, when her influence on John Lennon was first unfairly blamed for his gradual withdrawal from the group, leading to its eventual break-up. She was born in Tokyo, Japan in 1933, and moved with her parents to New York in 1947. There, she gained a minor reputation in the early 1960s for her poems, experimental films, and performance "happenings." Lennon met her in London, England in 1966, at the art gallery Indica, when she did not speak, but only handed him a card bearing the word "Breathe."

According to Sir Paul McCartney: "I introduced Yoko to John through my own interest in the avant-garde.... She was doing a thing for John Cage in New York.... I said 'I've got this friend, who might be able to interest you....' Maybe if I hadn't done that there might not have been this sort of huge period between them."

Lennon at that time was still married, living with his wife Cynthia in Weybridge, southern England, but he soon became besotted with Yoko. "As she was talking to me, I'd get high, and the discussion would get to such a level, I'd be getting higher and higher. Then she'd leave, and I'd go back to this sort of suburbia." It was not long before the couple were living together, and, when it became obvious that Yoko was pregnant, Cynthia obtained a divorce in November 1968.

On March 20, 1969—nine days after Paul McCartney's marriage to Linda Eastman—John and Yoko, dressed in crumpled white, were married secretly at the British consulate in Gibraltar. Then they flew to Paris, France, to face the press. "We're going to stage many happenings and events together," said Yoko. "This marriage was one of them." When the couple moved on to Amsterdam, they announced that they intended to stay in bed for a week. Photographers flocked to their hotel, hoping to find them naked, but were downcast to find them merely sitting up in bed, surrounded by notices reading "Bed Peace" and "Hair Peace."

"The men from the press Said: 'We wish you success,' I said 'We're only trying to get us some peace, Christ, you know it ain't easy...'" (from "The Ballad of John and Yoko.")

Columbia Takeover

Columbia is one of the oldest major universities in the United States, set in a northern part of New York City. From 1965 onward, the university began to expand with little concern for the local community, and plans for a new gymnasium provoked protests, not only from residents, but from the students themselves. This was but one factor in the uprising that took place in April 1968; another was the close link between the university and the Institute of Defense Analysis (I.D.A.). Columbia's president, Grayson Kirk, was on the board of I.D.A., and boasted of the military defense money that came to the university—something that enraged the members of Students for a Democratic Society (S.D.S.), who were strongly opposed to the continuing war in Vietnam.

In 1967, Kirk instituted a ban on all indoor demonstrations, and in April 1968 he placed six students who had protested against the I.D.A. connection—the "I.D.A. six"—on probation. On April 23, supporters of the six gathered in the main campus and, as night fell, they occupied Hamilton Hall and took the acting dean, Henry Coleman, hostage. By morning, five buildings had been occupied, and the S.D.S. took over Kirk's office.

At first the police were not brought in, and order was maintained by a group of faculty members who were broadly sympathetic to the students. For a week the university was at a standstill, as students took over further buildings. Then, soon after midnight on April 30, buses brought more than 1,000 uniformed and plainclothes police to the campus, while others entered university buildings through underground tunnels. Groups of police charged into Columbia, violently removing students, and even attacking bystanders. Several hundred students, and even academics, were severely injured, and there were 705 arrests.

Concessions were made, and the university returned temporarily to normal. But S.D.S. supporters were disciplined, and on May 13 they reoccupied Hamilton Hall. This time, police brutality was worse. Two students were hurled through plate glass, and in all 51 students and 17 police required hospital treatment. But in the end the students won acceptance of many of their demands—and president Kirk resigned.

During a graduation ceremony, a Columbia professor raises his arm to make a peace sign, and thus show solidarity with his students, who were protesting the Vietnam War.

De Gaulle Resigns

April 27, 1969: The curtain falls on Charles de Gaulle. After calling a national referendum on relatively minor issues that he was convinced were essential constitutional reforms, and receiving a strong "no" vote, de Gaulle interpreted this public rebuke as a lack of confidence in him, and the following day resigned as president of France. It was the end of an epoch.

De Gaulle had led the Free French forces against Germany throughout World War II (1939–1945), and had briefly served as French prime minister, before resigning in 1946. In May 1958, when army leaders in Algeria defied the French government's attempt to give the African nation independence, and France seemed on the verge of civil war, he had been recalled from retirement, and was elected president of the Fifth Republic, with widespread popular support, in December.

De Gaulle saw France through a stormy decade: he masterminded French withdrawal from Algeria, he brought an end to the riots of May 1968 by undermining the solidarity between workers and students in order to isolate the latter, and he personally handled the financial crisis of November 1968, when he made the decision not to devalue the franc. And in 1963 he had vetoed Britain's entry into the European Common Market. Behind his rather haughty façade, de Gaulle was surprisingly self-deprecating, once likening himself to the cartoon character Tintin, "a little man against the world." He always found the presidency a daunting task: "How can one govern a country," he complained in 1962, "that has 246 varieties of cheese?"

After his resignation, at the age of 78, de Gaulle retired to his modest home, la Boisserie, near the village of Colombey-les-deux-Eglises, and devoted most of his time to writing his memoirs. In May, escaping the electoral campaign that brought the election of his old ally Georges Pompidou, he took the opportunity to visit Ireland, the birthplace of his maternal ancestors, with his wife, Yvonne.

Charles de Gaulle died at his home on November 12, 1970. His very private funeral service was held in the village church where he had worshiped for much of his life, and his body was laid to rest in the tiny churchyard.

De Gaulle leaves the polling station in his home village in northern France, after casting his own vote in the referendum he had called on constitutional reforms.

British Royal Investiture

In a solemn ceremony held at Caernarfon Castle, north Wales, on July 1, 1969, Prince Charles, the eldest son of Queen Elizabeth II of England, was invested as Prince of Wales. He became the 21st holder of the title. The first incumbent was the future Edward II, the eldest surviving son of Edward I, who was granted it in 1301. Although the title is traditionally given to the male heir presumptive, it is not a birthright but the gift of the monarch.

The Queen gave Charles the title in 1957, when he was nine years old, but she let it be known that he would not be formally invested until he was of an age to understand its full significance. When the time came, he was approaching his 21st birthday. Some 4,000 guests assembled within the walls of the medieval castle, thousands of other people waited outside, and the event was televised live.

As constable of the castle, the Earl of Snowdon—former photographer Tony Armstrong-Jones, the husband of Princess Margaret—directed proceedings. The Queen invested the Prince with the insignia of his principality, and the earldom of Chester: a ceremonial sword, coronet, mantle, gold ring, and gold rod. In his formal response, the Prince declared: "I, Charles, Prince of Wales, do become your liege man of life and limb, and of earthly worship and faith and truth I will bear unto you, to live and die against all manner of folks."

In preparation for the event, Charles had spent some months studying the Welsh language, and—after a loyal address from the people of Wales read by Sir Ben Bowen Thomas, president of the University College of Wales—the Prince replied in both Welsh and English. He spoke of the long history of Wales and its determination to guard its own heritage: "A heritage that dates back into the mists of ancient British history, that has produced many brave men, princes, poets, bards, scholars, and, more recently, great singers, a very memorable 'Goon,' and eminent film stars...." He said he would involve himself as much as possible in the life of the principality.

After a brief religious service—again, in both English and Welsh—the Queen and her husband, Prince Philip, Duke of Edinburgh, led the Prince to a gate overlooking the Castle Square, and there presented him to the expectant crowds below.

This snapshot captures an affectionate look exchanged by Queen Elizabeth II and Prince Charles as they walk through Caernarfon Castle straight after the investiture ceremony.

Man on the Moon

"That's one small step for a man, one giant leap for mankind." With these words, at 10.56 p.m., Eastern Daylight Time on July 21, 1969, American astronaut Neil Armstrong stepped down from the Apollo 11 landing-craft Eagle onto the surface of the Moon in the area named the Sea of Tranquillity. At that moment, back on Earth, millions of TV viewers stood and cheered this amazing technological achievement.

Some minutes later, Armstrong was joined by his fellow astronaut, Colonel Edwin "Buzz" Aldrin, Jr., and the two men struggled to plant a mast with the Stars and Stripes (the flag had to be stiffened to stand out, for there is, of course, no wind on the Moon). Then, after some cautious initial steps, Armstrong and Aldrin began to bound across the surface, delightedly exploiting the lack of gravity. They set up scientific instruments, including a laser beam reflector, a seismometer that later transmitted evidence of a moonquake, and a sheet of aluminum foil to trap solar wind particles. They also collected 53.61 pounds of rock samples, and—like any tourist in a strange land—took photographs.

Relayed from Mission Control in Houston, Texas, President Nixon spoke to the Apollo crew: "Neil and Buzz, I am talking to you by telephone from the Oval Office of the White House, and this certainly has to be the most historic telephone call ever made.... Because of what you have done, the heavens have become a part of man's world. As you talk to us from the Sea of Tranquillity, it inspires us to redouble our efforts to bring peace and tranquillity to Earth...."

Neil Armstrong—first out and last back into the Lunar Module—spent 2 hours and 13 minutes outside. On returning to the Eagle, he and Aldrin took off their heavy boots and backpacks, and threw them out onto the Moon's surface, together with empty food packages and full urine bags. Twenty hours later they lifted off to rejoin the orbiting spacecraft, Columbia, piloted by Lt. Col. Michael Collins. "I was concentrating on the computers," reported Aldrin, "but I looked up long enough to see the flag fall over...." The three men splashed down safely in the Pacific Ocean off Hawaii on July 24. America was triumphant: the Russians had been beaten in the race to be the first nation to put a man on the Moon.

One of the few photographs showing Neil Armstrong on the surface of the Moon—most of the famous shots were taken by Armstrong of his fellow astronaut Buzz Aldrin.

Chappaquiddick

Edgartown is on Martha's Vineyard in Massachusetts. Every summer, the local yacht club held a regatta that was regularly attended by members of the Kennedy family. The family's parties were notorious. The 1966 celebration was described as "riotous," and in 1967 a rented cottage was left "a shambles." The assassination of Robert Kennedy in 1968 had kept the family away, but in 1969 two Kennedy boats were entered in the races. Teddy Kennedy—"the last of the Kennedys," who was said to have ambitions to run for President—decided that the weekend provided an opportunity for a party to reunite the "Boiler Room Girls," the former members of Bobby's campaign staff.

The party was made up of six men, including Kennedy's cousin Joe Gargan, and six girls, and was held in a cottage Gargan had rented on Chappaquiddick, a small island separated from the mainland by a narrow channel, and accessible only by a ferry that operated between 7.30 a.m. and midnight. Late on the evening of July 18, Kennedy left the party with 28-year-old ex-boiler room girl Mary Jo Kopechne, and drove his car off a wooden bridge on a track leading to the beach, drowning his passenger. He then swam to the mainland and went to bed in his hotel, failing to report the accident for 10 hours. At one time, it appears, he tried to claim that Mary Jo had been alone in the car. An unpublished police report suggested that she had remained alive for nearly two hours after the accident, trapped in a bubble of air.

Following the death of Bobby Kennedy, *Time* magazine reported that Teddy had been drinking heavily, and was "a deeply troubled man." Later inquiries revealed that he had committed several driving offenses as a young man, and that his license had not been renewed for five months before the tragedy on Chappaquiddick. However, none of this emerged at the inquest on Mary Jo. The "power of the Kennedys" went into operation, and in April 1970 it was announced that Teddy would face no legal action.

Even today, no one knows exactly what happened on the night of Mary Jo Kopechne's death, but the doubts cast a lasting shadow over the character and reputation of Senator Edward Kennedy, and put paid to his hopes of the presidency.

Teddy Kennedy's car is pulled from the water into which it careened off a bridge in the early hours of July 19, 1969. The body of a young woman was found dead in the back seat.

The Manson Murders

August 9, 1969: A housekeeper arriving for work at a home in the Bel Air district of Los Angeles, California, found the bodies of two men and a young woman shot and stabbed in the driveway. Inside the house, pregnant Sharon Tate, actress wife of film director Roman Polanski, lay dead in a pool of blood, and nearby was the body of a third man. "War," and "Pig" had been daubed in blood on the walls.

Three days earlier, a hippie musician, who lived in a commune at Spahn Ranch on the outskirts of Los Angeles, had been arrested for the murder of music teacher Gary Hinman. Hinman had been stabbed, and "Political Piggy" written in blood on his wall. Even when another similar murder was discovered on August 10, the police did not realize the connection with the Bel Air killings.

Two months later police from a small town more than 200 miles north of Los Angeles raided a ranch above Death Valley, and arrested a crowd calling themselves the Manson Family. Hiding in a cupboard they found the hippies' leader, a short, unimpressive figure, long-haired and bearded, who gave his name as "Manson, Charles M., a.k.a. Jesus Christ, God." Gradually, the truth emerged.

Manson, born in Cincinnati, Ohio, in 1934, arrived in San Francisco, California, in 1967, having spent the previous 12 years in prison on various charges. He discovered that he could exert an uncanny influence over the "flower children" of the time, and soon had a large following. Eventually, the Family had settled at Spahn Ranch in August 1968. Manson preached that the black population would soon kill all the whites in a terrible war, which he named Helter Skelter (from a number on The Beatles' *White Album* of 1968). Believing that he could set off this race war by a series of mindless killings, he had sent his followers on a rampage of slaughter. After his arrest, he boasted to fellow prisoners that he and the Family had murdered at least 35 people.

The trial of Manson, and six of his "family" opened in July 1970. All seven were found guilty, and sentenced to death. Manson told the court: "Ha, I'm already dead, have been all my life. I don't care anything about any of you." Two years later, the death penalty was abolished in California, and the sentences were commuted to life.

Two months after his arrest, Charles Manson turns away from an army of press
photographers as he waits to go into a pretrial hearing at the Los Angeles Hall of Justice.

Riots in the Bogside

In some ways, the situation in Ireland after 1920 could be compared to that in Germany, Korea, and Vietnam in the 1950s: a former single state, with a people united by a common language and a common cultural heritage, was divided in two. The division here, however, was not primarily political, but religious: the Irish Republic was predominantly, and constitutionally, Roman Catholic; Northern Ireland, comprising six of the nine counties that had made up the former province of Ulster, remained part of the United Kingdom, and was dominated by Protestants.

The Irish Republican Army (I.R.A.), which had gone underground after being outlawed by the Republic in 1936, carried out sporadic terrorist attacks against the British for some years, but by 1962 it was unwilling to be involved in further sectarian conflict in Northern Ireland and declared a ceasefire. However, the Protestant Ulster Volunteer Force (U.V.F.) began to terrorize Catholic residents of Belfast in 1966, and in 1969 a new "Provisional" I.R.A. was formed.

There were, of course, political connotations. Many Catholics—discriminated against in work, social conditions, and politics—dreamed of reunification with the Republic; Protestants feared the introduction of reforms that threatened their privileges. In January 1969, Protestants attacked a civil rights' march from Belfast to Londonderry (or Derry, as the Catholics call it). That night, sectarian rioting broke out in the area of Derry known as the Bogside.

Among the most inflammatory events each summer are the marches mounted by the Protestant "Orange Orders" to commemorate the siege of Derry in 1689, and the defeat of Catholic forces at the Battle of the Boyne in 1690. In 1969, there were clashes in towns across Northern Ireland, and on August 12, as the "Apprentice Boys" marched through the center of Derry and past the Bogside, they were attacked. The Royal Ulster Constabulary (R.U.C.), the Protestant-dominated local police force, failed to control the violence, and two days later the British army was brought in to restore order. Troops were destined to remain in the province for more than a quarter of a century. Although a peace process is now under way, the so-called Irish question remains unresolved.

Roman Catholic rioters photographed in the Bogside of Londonderry, Northern Ireland, on August 12, 1969. They are throwing petrol bombs at armored cars belonging to the R.U.C.

The Weathermen

In the late 1960s, urban violence became a vehicle of protest in Europe, and various leftist organizations—particularly, but not exclusively, those that opposed the war in Vietnam—began to advocate its use in the United States. One such group was the Weathermen, led by "gangly, cold, foul-mouthed" Mark Rudd. Their name came from their original manifesto, which was headed with a line from the Bob Dylan song "Subterranean Homesick Blues": "You don't need a weatherman to know which way the wind blows."

The Weathermen first emerged as a result of events at the June 1968 convention of Students for a Democratic Society (S.D.S.) in Chicago, Illinois. The S.D.S., which coincided with the Democratic convention in the same city at which the party nominated Hubert Humphrey as its presidential candidate, featured a whole range of political dissidents. Many of them were harmless eccentrics, but even the most vicious did not deserve the brutal treatment they received when they thronged the streets of the downtown area. Mayor Richard Daley sent in 12,000 police, who clubbed and gassed demonstrators with alarming and needless ferocity.

This outrage radicalized the Weathermen. Over the next year they laid plans for a campaign of terrorism, and, shortly before midnight on October 6, 1969, as the curtain-raiser to their "Days of Rage," they blew up a memorial to Chicago policemen in the city's Haymarket Square. In the days that followed, they wrecked cars and smashed windows in the business district. More than 300 persons were arrested, and a police official declared: "We now feel that it is kill or be killed."

The Weathermen then joined forces with Revolutionary Force 9 to carry out a series of bombings in New York. They also attacked the Pentagon and the Capitol in Washington, D.C. Vast damage was caused to property, and there were almost 50 deaths, but most of those killed were Weathermen, who blew themselves up while manufacturing explosives. After raids by police and federal agents in late 1969, most of the Weathermen were arrested, and those who remained went underground. Although there were some further incidents in the early 1970s, the November roundups were the last knockings of the New Left in the United States.

November 19, 1969: An officer in Cambridge, Massachusetts, arrests a member of the Weathermen as police crack down on the militant anarchist group.

Woodstock and Altamont

The best, and the worst, of the giant pop music events effectively closed the turbulent decade of the 1960s. The hugely successful Woodstock Music and Arts Fair ("An Aquarian Exposition") was followed, within four months, by the chaos and mayhem of the Altamont Festival.

Held in August 1969 near Bethel, in upstate New York, Woodstock was described by *Time* magazine as "history's largest happening… one of the significant political and social events of the age." Many of the most "significant" performers of the time were absent, however: there were no Beatles or Rolling Stones, no Bob Dylan, no Doors—although Joan Baez, Janis Joplin, Jimi Hendrix, and the Who, among others, appeared. But over a quarter million happy fans—dubbing themselves the "Woodstock Nation"—painted their faces, tripped, stripped, and indulged in open-air sex, fed from the stands of Food for Love and the Hog Farmers, and (relatively) peacefully enjoyed the music of 30 bands and soloists.

Closing the festival, Max Yasgur, on whose farm it was held, declared: "This is the largest group of people ever to have assembled in one place…. I think you people have proven something to the world—that a half a million kids can get together and have fun and music, and nothing but fun and music."

But everything went sour at Altamont Speedway, in the Bay Area of San Francisco, California, in December. Flushed with the success of their current U.S. tour, The Rolling Stones announced that they would stage a free concert, their plan being to shoot sufficient footage to complete a movie of the tour. After two other venues had proved impractical, and with only a day to go, the Altamont proprietor offered his disused and decrepit site. Unwisely, he took the advice of The Grateful Dead, and hired Hell's Angels to guard the stage.

The Stones arrived by helicopter, deliberately late, by which time the "guards," already drunk and high on drugs, had begun beating up members of the audience. As Mick Jagger launched into "Sympathy for the Devil," the singer thought he saw one of the crowd point a gun at him. Within seconds, the unfortunate Meredith Hunter had been beaten and stabbed to death. It was the end of the 1960s' dream.

The Jimi Hendrix Experience live on stage at Woodstock in August. By the end of the year, the 1960s were over, not just literally, but also spiritually.

Index